INST.

MW01617044

STRATEGIES

····· THAT WORK ·····

Pat Quinn
The RTI Guy

Instructional Strategies that Work

Pat Quinn

Copyright© 2013 Pat Quinn
ISBN 9780-9838516-5-3

JULIANJOHN

JulianJohn Publishing

Cover Design by Sean O'Connor
OhSeeDesign.com

Printed in the United States of America

••• TABLE OF CONTENTS •••

FIVE INSTRUCTIONAL STRATEGIES THAT DEVELOP SUCCESSFUL LEARNERS

• • • Carmen Ervin • • •

SCHOOLS ACROSS THE NATION have the challenge of educating the largest number of diverse students in previous history. Many practices and theories are used to guide a teacher's instruction, and there are many obstacles educators face today. Demographics have changed, family dynamics have changed, and school districts have enforced mandates that put a strain on the educational system as a whole. All of these issues contribute to the educational focus today.

A student's success and academic fulfillment is impacted by the ability to successfully access the curriculum. In the early history, teaching instruction was a one-size-fits-all approach. Today, changes had to be made due to the demands that school districts place on educators for all learners to leave educational systems with the skills to fulfill a comfortable lifestyle, one that allows them to be major society contributors. Due to current research and studies, this has been a challenge to accomplish. There are students who enter post-secondary systems with insufficient skills to survive on that level.

So today's educators have the challenge to make successful students out of every learner who enters our schools. This demand has continuously become a major topic of debate and the focus of many educational articles and journals. This topic has also been a major concern for the educational system, both nationwide and locally. As educators, we are encouraged to make instruction meaningful and enjoyable for all learners. Just as our appearances differ, so do our students' needs. The current focus is on providing each individual learner with the design needed to bring about academic success.

According to research, one major point that determines how successful the student becomes is impacted by learning readiness and instruction received upon entering school. Therefore, early intervention instruction has a major impact on the success of our students. After this process has been implemented, we have the challenge of maintaining and increasing growth in learning. This can only be accomplished through educators who are properly trained and have a passion for making learning meaningful, appropriate, and intentional.

Now we will journey into effective instructional techniques and strategies. This can only be accomplished if each education team member—be it teacher, support personnel, administration, school boards, superintendents, lawmakers, and community—embraces this awesome quote,

> "What we need to do is learn to work in the system, by which I mean that everybody, every team, every platform, every division, every component is there not for individual competitive profit or recognition, but for contribution to the system as a whole on a win-win basis." – W. Edwards Deming

As teachers, we are only effective when we consider planning based on the outcome we envision for our students. This can only be accomplished through continuous research and study on classroom environment and learning styles of the students. In this chapter, we will address different instructional techniques and strategies.

There are five instructional techniques that are practiced on a regular basis in the classroom, with specific strategies that have proven to be successful in developing successful learners, regardless of academic level. The techniques are direct instruction, indirect instruction, interactive instruction, experiential learning, and independent study. Each technique will be addressed individually and culminated with a chart that provides examples of strategies and differentiated strategies that can be used to include every learner.

Direct Instruction

Direct instruction is a technique used to present a lesson, and it is more teacher directed. Direct instruction is a way of providing information or developing step-by-step skills. This technique is believed to be the easiest to implement and requires only minimal participation from the learner. This technique is considered by most to be the least effective way to reach all learners. According to a study called **Project Follow Through** which was conducted in 1970's, direct instruction dramatically improved cognitive skills among a group of students who received direct instruction as a means for presenting lessons.

Indirect Instruction

Indirect instruction is the next technique used and is more student focused. Lessons using this technique are high on student involvement. When using this technique, the learner has several opportunities to use their own curiosity and find nontraditional ways to solve a problem or figure out an answer.

Interactive Instruction

Interactive instruction involves the use of collaboration among the students. Students are grouped to gather learning from each other and take responsibility for their own learning. This approach to learning tends to lean heavily on sharing knowledge. Research suggests that this technique alone shows that students are engaged at the highest level, and it has been proven to be the most effective way of closing the gap in academic achievement.

Experiential Learning

This technique focuses on the individual student's learning process. Experiential learning is considered a powerful tool for learning. The learner must have strong self-initiative. Experiential learning produces high retention and better understanding of material. Finally, the learner has a high level of motivation when using this technique because they have the opportunity to teach their peers what has been learned.

Independent Study

This final technique is different from the other techniques in that the students may work in small groups, but the tasks are done independently. Independent study allows the learner to become more efficient as an individual student by developing initiative, self-improvement, and self-reliance. It allows for flexibility in the learning environment, and one or more learners can participate at one time.

While a brief description has been given for each technique, more useful information is included in the following table to outline each technique and provide examples and strategies for implementing each in the classroom.

Chart 1.1
Instructional Teaching Techniques and Strategies

Instructional Techniques	Examples/Strategies	Differentiated Instructional Strategies
Direct Instruction	• Reading a book • Displaying a diagram • Showing real-life examples of subject matter • Watching a movie	• Listen to an audio tape • Label a diagram • Dialogue about a topic • Look for ideas from nature

	• PowerPoint presentation • Drill and practice	• Describe sequence or process
Indirect Instruction	• Problem solving • Case studies • Compare/contrast • Inquiry • Concept mapping	• Create a tableau • Solve a problem together • Survey/interview others • Examine materials • Classify/rank or compare
Interactive Instruction	• Debates • Role playing • Peer practice • Problem solving • Panels	• Write a play • Develop a mime • Compose a rap song or rhyme • Interpret evidence • Discuss and come to conclusion
Experiential Learning	• Field trips • Simulations • Games • Surveys • Field observations	• Work through a simulation • Make a connection with past information or experiences • Illustrate an event • Write in a journal • Develop or experiment
Independent Study	• Essays • Learning activity package • Reports • Learning centers • Computer-assisted instruction	• Paint or design a poster • Think about and plan • Create a poem or recitation

Finally, all educators know that students do not learn in the same way; therefore, different methods and strategies are needed in order for them to be successful learners. It is the role of an effective teacher to have clear directions of each student's learning process, academic level, and individual learning style. When each of these steps have been adequately researched and planned, the strategies used will ensure that the educational plan will be effective and the student will experience success.

SIX INSTRUCTIONAL STRATEGIES TO PROMOTE STUDENT THINKING

• • • Jonily Zupancic • • •

THE OLD PROVERB "YOU can lead a horse to water, but you can't make it drink" also applies to students and their learning. We can lead them to knowledge, but we can't make them learn. So, don't try to make kids learn, make them think—or in other words, make them thirsty. There are six ways to provide a means of entering into students' minds and developing their thinking. Once we unlock the potential of student thought, they gain greater access to learning the content.

#1 Set the Stage

Begin with a situation to explore and problems to solve. Give students a context or situation. Tell them from the beginning what they are to think about. Provide students opportunities to make sense of the situation before beginning to question. By asking too many questions too quickly, we limit potential opportunities for thinking.

- *Jesse and Kay:* Jesse starts with $50 and gets $5 each day. Kay has no money today, but gets $7 per day.

- *Paint:* Jim can paint a room in 8 hours, and Sally can paint the same size room in 4 hours.

- *Candy:* 80 candies are shared by two boys in the ratio of 2:3.

- *Rosa:* Rosa can count to 100 in one minute.

- *Square Pizzas:* Pizza Palace only makes square pizzas, but of many sizes. Once the pizzas are cut into pieces, the number of pieces in each row is the same as the number of pieces in each column.

- *Painted Cube:* A cube with a side length of 10 cm is painted on all sides.

#2 Ask Questions

Questions can assess what students know and don't know, but questions should also be a vehicle to take student understanding to a deeper level. If students already know the answers to the questions teachers are asking, then those questions do not promote thinking. Students must be provided with questions that require a deeper level of understanding—in other words, questions they are not able to solve immediately. There are a variety of question formats to emphasize during this process. For example:

Student-Created Questions

Again, it is important for the students to have time to make sense of the situation. One strategy that allows students to more fully understand the situation is to create their own questions. Begin by asking students, "What math questions can be created for this situation?"

General Questions

General questions can be used with any situation or problem.

- What do you notice?
- What patterns are there?
- Why?
- How do you know?
- What do you think?
- What more can you tell me?
- What else could you explore?
- What would a picture or graph look like?

Problem-Specific Questions

Problem-specific questions are directly related to the situation at hand. Not only are these questions customized to the situation, but they are designed to challenge all levels of understanding. These types of questions have the potential to differentiate instruction by scaffolding and enriching, as well as providing intervention.

Jesse and Kay: Jesse starts with $50 and gets $5 each day. Kay has no money today, but gets $7 per day.

- How do Jesse and Kay's money situations compare?
- Who starts with more money?
- How much more money does Jesse start with?
- How much does each of them have on day 7?
  o Who has more on day 7?
  o How much more?
- How much does each have on day 43?
  o Who has more on day 43?
  o How much more?
- On what day will Jesse and Kay have the same amount of money?
- If Jesse starts with $300 and loses $5 each day, and Kay starts with no money, but still earns $7 per day, on what day will they have the same amount of money?

Paint: Jim can paint a room in 8 hours, and Sally can paint the same size room in 4 hours.

- How much of the room can Sally paint in one hour?
- How much of the room can Sally and Jim paint together in one hour?
- How much of the room can Jim paint by himself in 7 hours?
- Who paints more of a room in two hours?
  o How much more?
- How many rooms can Jim paint in a 40-hour work week?

- Who should earn more money per hour, Jim or Sally? Why?
- If Jim and Sally work together to paint one room, how long will it take?
- Jim and Sally improve their efficiency. Jim can now paint a room in 6 hours, and Sally can paint the same size room in 3 hours. How long will it take them to paint one room if they work together?

Candy: 80 candies are shared by two boys in the ratio of 2:3.

- Which boy starts with more candy?
- How much candy does boy 1 get at each distribution?
- What is the rate at which boy 2 gets candy?
- How many candies does boy 1 have after the 12th round?
- What part of the total candies does boy 1 get?
- How many candies does each boy get if all 80 pieces are distributed?
    - o   Are there any candies left over?
- On what round will the boys have the same number of pieces of candy?
- What total fraction of the candies does each boy get?
    - o   What percent?
- If there are still 80 candies and 2 boys, what ratios are possible so that, after all rounds, no candies are left over?
- If the ratio is still 2:3, how many total candies are possible to share between 2 boys if there will be no candies left over?
- If there are 120 candies shared between 2 boys in the ratio 3:5, how many candies will each boy get?

Rosa: Rosa can count to 100 in one minute.

- What is Rosa's rate?
- How long will it take her to count to one million?
- How many 100's are in 1,000?
- How many 1,000's are in 1,000,000?

- How many 100's are in a million?
- How many numbers can Rosa count in 10 minutes? 20 minutes?
- How many numbers can Rosa count in 100 minutes?
- How many hours is 100 minutes?
- What decimal of an hour is 4 minutes?
- What fraction of an hour is 4 minutes? What percent?
- How long will it take her to count to a billion? A trillion?

Square Pizzas: Pizza Palace only makes square pizzas, but of many sizes. Once the pizzas are cut into pieces, the number of pieces in each row is the same as the number of pieces in each column.

- How many pieces would a pizza have with a side length of 3?
- How many pieces would a pizza have with a side length of 10?
- If a pizza could be large enough, how many pieces would a pizza have with a side length of 123?
- How many pieces would a pizza have with side length n?
- For a pizza with side length 5 units, how many corner pieces (pieces with 2 sides of crust) are there?
- For a pizza with side length 7, how many edge pieces (pieces with one side of crust) are there?
- For a pizza with side length 4, how many center pieces (pieces with no crust) are there?
- What is the pattern of increase for edge pieces in pizzas from side length 2 through side length 10?
- How many edge pieces are there in a pizza with side length n?
- What is the area (measured in pizza slices) of a pizza with side length 9?
- What is the perimeter of a pizza with side length 9 units?
  - o How many pizza slice units of crust?

Painted Cube: A cube with a side length of 10 cm is painted on all sides.

- If the cube with a side length of 10 units was broken into 1 by 1 by 1 unit cubes, how many unit cubes would there be? Why?
- What fraction of a cube with side length 10 cm is a cube with side length 5?
- How many 5 by 5 by 5 cubes fit into a 10 by 10 by 10 cube?
- How many unit cubes make a cube of side length 3 units?
- How many unit cubes have paint on them in a cube with side length 10?
- How many unit cubes have paint on 3 sides (corner pieces) in a cube with side length 10?
- How many center pieces (unit cubes with no paint) are there in a cube with side length 5 units?
- How many edge pieces (unit cubes with paint on 2 sides) are there in a cube with side length 8 units?
- How many face pieces (unit cubes with paint on 2 sides) are there in a cube with side length 6 pieces?
- In a cube of side length 6 units, what is the ratio of edge pieces to center pieces?
- If all of the unit cubes from a cube with side length 5 were put into a bag, what is the probability of pulling a corner piece?
- What is the volume of a cube with side length 7 units?
- What is the surface area of a cube with side length 7 units?
- If the surface area of a cube is 600 square units, what is the volume?
- Is the surface area of a cube with side length 5 units the same as the number of unit cubes with paint? Why or why not?

- If the volume of a rectangular prism is 64 cubic units, what are possible whole number lengths?

#3 Provide Time

It is critical that teachers give students time to reflect, think, and work in order to fully explore the depth of each question. It is also helpful to have students talk and think out loud to each other before presenting their solutions and answers to the class. Be patient, not all students at the end of "think time" are going to arrive at the same level of understanding. When this strategy of providing time becomes common practice, the results of student thinking and developing understanding will increase and improve.

#4 Encourage Thought

Tell students they are great thinkers. The more students hear this statement, the more they will believe it and the more they will take the risk to open their minds to think. By prefacing questions with "this is difficult," and not "this one is easy," students will not be as afraid to make a mistake because there is no shame in answering difficult questions incorrectly. If students can't answer what we consider to be an "easy" question, then why would they attempt a more complicated problem? Teachers should promote a culture of thinking and learning in which all students can take risks, be wrong, and still feel successful.

#5 Involve Everyone

We want children to take risks; therefore, it is imperative to establish an atmosphere of acceptance. This climate will allow even the weaker students to feel comfortable enough to participate and learn, while simultaneously maintaining the engagement and interest of higher-level students.

#6 Listen Actively

There is nothing more devastating to a child than working up the courage to speak in front of the class, only to be diminished or ignored. Teachers need to be actively listening to student thinking and documenting student understandings and misunderstandings. Active listening by teachers is the key to ongoing, frequent formative assessment. Teachers can show that they are listening by making eye contact, commenting on student answers, and asking follow-up questions to the class. Teachers can react to correct, as well as incorrect, answers in the same way and by saying, "That was a very interesting statement. Would anyone like to add to that thought?" Follow-up questions can generate additional student thinking, as well as discussions of whether or not answers are correct.

Teachers need to provide strategies that help students actively listen to one another. In order to accomplish this goal, tell the students that they will randomly be selected to repeat the answer given by their classmate. Refrain from repeating the response yourself. When students begin to realize that the teacher is not going to repeat an answer given by their classmate and they may be called upon, there is a higher level of engagement and motivation to listen to one another's thinking.

Turn Thinking into Learning

"I cannot teach anyone anything; I can only make them think"–Socrates. Don't focus only on the content itself. Remember, we cannot force a child to learn, we can only inspire him to think. Teachers should spend time creating problems and questions, encouraging students, and providing time for students to think, participate, and listen. Strive to make students thirsty, and everyone learns.

INSTRUCTIONAL TEACHING TECHNIQUES AND STRATEGIES TEACHERS USE TO MOTIVATE STUDENTS

• • • Dr. Lilia O. Burton, Ed.D • • •

Know Your Classroom Learners

IT IS ALWAYS A good practice to know each student in your classroom. Determine the students' individual learning styles. The best time to determine their individual learning styles is at the beginning of the school year. One way to determine the students' individual learning styles is through student observation during classroom interaction with other students. Another way to determine students' individual learning styles is through conversations with their parents during open house and classroom visits. Furthermore, you can determine individual learning styles by casual talks with other teachers, including their previous teachers, during staff meetings, in the teachers' lounge, and during lunch. The determination process of your students' learning styles should not take longer than thirty minutes. You should observe your students several times to ascertain that your teaching styles work best for each individual learner.

Small-Group Instruction

Diverse learners have different ways of learning. Differentiated instruction is an effective teaching technique that works in small-group instruction because it provides opportunities for teachers to teach students based on their learning styles, age-appropriate abilities, and levels of understanding. An effective size group for small-group instruction is four to five students. Teaching and learning should be flexible to allow students time and mastery of new skills at their own pace.

Differentiated instruction is also an effective teaching technique that works well in small -group intervention. English language learners (ELs) and struggling learners benefit from small-group intervention because the delivery of instruction on a one-on-one basis is intensive, and the students focus on mastering targeted skills. In reading, small-group intervention should include phonemic awareness practice, such as letter/sound recognition, as well as blending and segmenting words. In mathematics, small-group instruction should include number facts from 0 to 20, as well as addition and subtraction practice.

Hands-On Learning

Seeing, touching, and manipulating real objects and manipulatives are other ways to teach students how to observe, investigate, and discover new things. Students are motivated to learn when they are having fun while working on new skills. Hands-on learning is an effective instructional strategy for students, especially ELs and struggling learners, because it gives them the opportunity to interact with each other and communicate about what they are learning. Teachers can utilize a hands-on learning strategy during writing, reading, math, science, and other core subjects. Examples of hands-on learning are as follows: During writing, teachers can use real objects, such as candy bars, to help students describe colors, sizes, and shapes. Students can also use the same objects to describe the taste. In reading, teachers can help students by allowing them to manipulate letters to spell a word or arrange the words to make a complete sentence. In math, teachers can use *Peanut M & M's* to classify the candies according to colors, count how many candies are in each color, and add all the numbers from each color to get the total numbers of candies. In science, teachers can use real seeds to study plants. Students will be able to learn responsibility as they plant their own seeds and observe and record daily the changes they see as the seed grows into a plant. Hands-on learning provides unlimited possibilities of meaningful activities, interactive discussions, and active learning.

Utilizing Technology in Your Classroom

The 20th century classroom is now equipped with computers. Every year, new programs and games are introduced. Some programs and games are updated versions of the old ones, others are offered on a trial basis, some are offered free in exchange for a pilot research, and some are paid for by individual schools or the school system. Students in the primary grades are now learning new skills with the use of computers as a teaching tool. Kindergarten students are taught how to use computers at the beginning of the school year. Students who are visual and auditory learners can benefit from using technology in the classroom. Intermediate and high school students become independent learners using computers for research projects, self-study, and receiving updates on world events and recent scientific discoveries. Additionally, the use of technology offers unlimited possibilities for analytical learners. Computers help reinforce the lesson being taught and the skills being learned.

Strategies for Vocabulary Retention

Are students expected to sit all day and listen to their teachers talk? How can teachers assist ELs and also help native English speakers understand the language used in their reading, math, science, and social studies classes? How can we help the struggling learners? In some classrooms, teachers talk most of the time and students listen for a few minutes of their time. In a general classroom setting, a teacher should not assume that students who are learning on their grade level already know the meaning of the word being introduced. Allow students to ask questions and have them explain their answers during discussions.

As any good teacher knows, diverse learners have different learning styles; therefore, a good strategy for vocabulary retention would be to introduce vocabulary words directly by using writing boards, technology, the dictionary, and/or word walls. Read each vocabulary word and teach it indirectly by using real life experiences, pictures, drawings, and manipulatives. Begin your lesson by introducing the topic and vocabulary words. Have your students discuss what they think the vocabulary words mean. The more vocabulary words students know, the better they understand what they read. Teachers should use pictures or real objects to give meanings to a word or group of words. Allowing students the opportunity to participate in a meaningful activity and a learning experience that involves their five senses would enhance their vocabulary retention. By using their five senses, students should be able to describe, give meaning, or have an image or idea of what the word means. In elementary grades, teachers should label pictures and objects. The more labeled pictures or real objects students see, the more words they accumulate to use in English language. The following activities are classroom strategies for vocabulary retention.

- Pre-teach vocabulary by using real objects, pictures, drawings, hand and facial gestures, role playing, etc. Teachers should not just read or tell students the meaning of the word. Students are more comfortable discussing the word meaning amongst themselves.

- Say the word, and say it again with the group. Ask one student to say the word and have the whole class repeat the word. Allow the students to act it out if they have to in order to understand the word meaning.

- Use graphic organizers to support students' newly acquired language skills, review vocabulary words daily, display vocabulary words on the word wall, and label drawings and pictures (in English and Spanish).

- Use computers, television, and audio or recorded books to improve their listening, speaking, reading, and writing skills. Allow students to again watch, listen, read, or review the skills being taught. Repetition is a good strategy to enhance vocabulary retention.

- Model the use of dictionaries and teach students how to use prefixes and suffixes to determine meaning. Most classrooms are now equipped with "Elmo" or "Robotics." Some teachers use overhead projectors, and others prefer worksheets to model the use of dictionaries. Teachers know their students best and know what strategy works best for them.

Assessment that Works

All classrooms have diverse learners with different personalities and learning styles, as all good teachers already know. It is common in every classroom to have students who quickly learn their skills and grasp the concept of what is being taught, while some struggle to understand the lesson and do not remain on task. Without assessments, the struggling learners will eventually fall off track. Given the students' differences, it is important to assess the students' knowledge of the topic or subject before presenting the lesson to make sure that an effective teaching strategy will be utilized to narrow the gap between the students.

Students are the best indicator of whether the teacher's teaching techniques and strategies are effective. Teachers, therefore, should assess their students often before each lesson, during the lesson, and after the lesson. Teachers can measure their students' levels of understanding by using formal and informal assessments. A combination of standardized tests, tests from the textbook being used, and teacher-created tests from the curriculum are examples of formal assessment. These assessments provide numerical or alphabetical scores or points for each correct answer. The results indicate a student's level of understanding in a given subject. Examples of informal assessments include observation, interviews, discussions, surveys, and students' participation.

• • •

References

Bunch, S. (2009). Retrieved (10/30/2010), http://www.suite
    101.com/content/esl-vocabulary-strategies article.

Colorín Colorado (2007). Vocabulary Development. Retrieved
    (8/28/2010), http://colorincolorado.com

Effective Teaching Methods in Elementary Public Schools. Retrieved
    (9/22/2012), http://www.ehow.com/way 5529755

Effective Teaching Strategies to Reach All Elementary Learners.
    Retrieved (9/22/2012), http://www.ehow.com/way 5760293

Schifferdanoff, V. (2005). Teaching ELL: Reading and Writing
    Strategies. Retrieved (8/28/2010), http://shop.scholastic.com

SEVEN RESEARCH-BASED INSTRUCTIONAL TECHNIQUES AND STRATEGIES FOR BUILDING STUDENTS' VOCABULARY

• • • Corinne Thompson • • •

Section 1: Introduction

THE ACT OF TEACHING vocabulary, on the surface, may appear to be easy, but it certainly requires knowledge of various teaching *techniques* and teaching *strategies* to be effective. Let's differentiate between the terms teaching *techniques* and teaching *strategy*. *Technique* is the tool you use to teach, and the *Strategy* is how skillfully you use the tool to achieve the objective. For example: If I want students to use and remember the word "delectable," I could use the technique of writing the word in sentences. However, instead of having students write random sentences, I could use RAFT Papers as the strategy to the writing process. This chapter is written to provide teachers with seven research-based practical *techniques* they can use to improve students' vocabulary development, and it also outlines some *strategies* I have used successfully in my own classroom. The scope of this chapter will not allow me to include all the resources I could share with you, so feel free to contact me by email (listed in my bio at the end of this chapter) for additional information.

It is sad, but true, that many students find learning vocabulary a boring chore. It does not have to be that way. One reason vocabulary instruction is not appealing to learners is the ineffective strategies teachers often use to present the task. The following list includes examples of isolated tasks many teachers assign in vocabulary instruction, which, on their own, are not very effective and motivating strategies.

a.   Using a dictionary to look up words

b.   Using written context alone to figure out word meanings

c.   Relying solely upon unplanned (teachable moments) to introduce new vocabulary

d.   Assigning weekly study lists of words

e.   Writing words in sentences

f.   Weekly tests on wordlists

g.   Using a thesaurus to help determine word meanings

h.   Using rote memorization for words and their meanings

Research has shown that, "Rote memorization of words and definitions is the least effective instructional method [of learning new vocabulary] resulting in little long-term effect" (Kameenui, Dixon and Carine, 1987; Baker, Simmoms, and Kameenui, 1995).

Section 2: What is Vocabulary?

According to Random House Webster's Unabridged Dictionary, vocabulary is defined as "the stock of words used by or known to a particular people or group of persons" (p. 2129, 2001). English Club defines vocabulary as "active vocabulary" and "passive vocabulary" (1997-2012). Active vocabulary comprises words you know, understand, and use in everyday speech. Passive vocabulary includes words you hear and though you may know them, they are not necessarily a part of your speaking or writing vocabulary. Vocabulary is a term that can also loosely mean the words teachers pick out of reading selections and use to pre-teach content. Furthermore, vocabulary can be specific to a certain occupation or branch of study. For example, certain words with prefixes and suffixes are predominantly related to the sciences and are derived from Greek or Latin. These words include: hypo-thermia, hetero-geneous, hyper-tension, and epi-dermis.

Vocabulary is one of the five big areas of reading in a model outlined by the National Reading Panel. The other four areas, namely Phonemic Awareness, Phonics, Fluency, and Comprehension, are closely connected to vocabulary. We could view these latter four as the building blocks of reading and view vocabulary as the cement that holds them all together. Without the cement, they all fall apart. In other words, the purpose of reading, writing, or conversing orally is to communicate. Language is expressive and receptive. The intent is that what is communicated will be understood by the receiver. Since vocabulary is the stock of words used to communicate, these words must be understood in order for communication to be meaningful. Vocabulary is developed mainly by listening and reading. J. K. Rowling says, "The most important thing is to read as much as you can, like I did. It will give you an understanding of what makes good writing, and it will enlarge your vocabulary" (Brainy Quote). I developed the following acronym to show the importance of expanding our vocabulary. The acronym reveals my personal views on vocabulary:

Vocabulary
Opens doors to
Conversations
And
Builds
Users'
Language
And
Reading comprehension skills
Yeah!

Section 3: Seven Research-based Instructional Techniques and Strategies for Teaching Vocabulary

Research has indicated that the way vocabulary traditionally has been taught needs to be changed. However, there are not many alternatives offered. Based on the research findings, the following are seven techniques for teaching vocabulary and some strategies I have employed in my classroom to develop a comprehensive vocabulary instruction program.

1. **Teachers should create opportunities for students to make connections to vocabulary words across content areas.**

    Studies have shown that, "Students develop their reading comprehension better when they can understand the nature of a word from multiple perspectives" (Boulware & Crow, 2008). Students need to encounter new vocabulary in various contexts in order for the words to become more meaningful to them. Stahl and Fairbanks state that, "Vocabulary knowledge increases when new words are encountered repeatedly in context through reading and listening" (1986). In order to compare new words with previously learned words, students need to be able to connect the new vocabulary words to situations they know of or have experienced. They need to manipulate these words in a variety of settings and take part in discussions about the various uses and meanings of words. According to Johnson, *et al.*, "Vocabulary knowledge increases when new words are connected with other words that are semantically related" (1986). In a document entitled "Vocabulary Instruction," it is cited that, "A knowledge of word roots and [affixes] helps students decipher new words, particularly if they connect the root to a word they know well. However, the memorization of long lists of roots and [affixes] is not productive" (Montgomery County Public Schools).

    The study of vocabulary across all content areas is very important if students are to comprehend the learning materials presented to them in order to become critical thinkers. Fred Frith commented that learning vocabulary is "... like learning a language; you can't speak a language fluently until you find out who you are in that language, and that has as much to do with your body as it does with vocabulary ..." (Brainy Quote).

2. Offer direct instruction in vocabulary.

Why teach vocabulary? The reason for explicitly teaching vocabulary is to help students increase word knowledge and be able to integrate the new words into their speaking, reading, and writing aspects of language. Marzano and colleagues point out that research provides a strong case for systematic instruction in vocabulary at virtually every grade level (Marzano *et al.*, 2001). In his book, *Classroom Instruction that Works,* Marzano points out five generalizations that can be used to guide instruction in vocabulary:

1. Students must encounter words in context more than once (at least six times) to learn them (p. 124).
2. Instruction in new words enhances learning those words in context (p. 126).
3. One of the best ways to learn a new word is to associate an image with it (p.126).
4. Direct vocabulary instruction works (p. 127).
5. Direct instruction on words that are critical to new content produces the most powerful learning (p.127).

Instruction in vocabulary should focus on building students' active vocabulary and passive vocabulary. The aim in teaching vocabulary should be to help students widen and add depth to their active vocabulary by transferring words from their passive vocabulary to their active vocabulary bank. Teachers can help students make this transference by incorporating those inactive words in classroom conversations as academic language. For example, students will hear the words *humidity* or *precipitation* on the radio or television in relationship to the weather. The teacher can deliberately use that word in class, such as saying to a group of first graders: "After recess, we will all have a refreshing drink at the water fountain because of the *humidity* outside today." Or on a rainy or snowy day, ask, "What is the *precipitation* outside today?" Evelyn Waugh says that, "One forgets words as one forgets names. One's vocabulary needs constant fertilizing or it will die" (Brainy Quote). Instructors can play a very vital role in helping students build and "fertilize" their vocabulary. They can use simple strategies, such as: guide students in correctly pronouncing the words; explain the meaning of the new word in language familiar to the students; connect the word to students' prior knowledge; give synonym/antonym for the new word; use the word or its derivative in sentences and other contexts; give examples of ways the word can be used; and model how the new word can replace formerly used common words, such as in the two examples that follow: The student's speech was *unprepared*. The student's speech was *extemporaneous*.

3. **Differentiate strategies and resources to cater to students' learning styles when teaching new words.**

   Teachers should allow students to encounter words in various situations which appeal to their visual, auditory, and kinesthetic sensory modalities. Students should be allowed opportunities to elaborate on word meanings by generating their own additional oral and written examples and visual representations of each new word. For vocabulary learning to be beneficial to students, they must see the word, not just hear it. For example, the words no and know are homophones, so the word in reference must me visual, also. Instruction in vocabulary should include direct teaching of individual words and also teaching students how to use various strategies when learning new words. These strategies include creating vocabulary study flashcards, writing vocabulary words in vocabulary notebook, and using context clues and word analysis (prefixes, suffixes, roots and base). When students look at roots, prefixes, and suffixes, they will understand how word parts are helpful in determining the meaning of a word (as well as its spelling).

Although vocabulary instruction is more than just looking up words in a dictionary, students should be able to use resources such as a dictionary, glossary, or thesaurus to confirm the meanings of words. Besides these resources, I have used several curriculums for vocabulary instruction. The list includes: *Academic Vocabulary* (Including the Six Plus 1 Traits), *Reading Drills*, *Vocabulary Drills*, *Making Words*, and *RAFT Papers*. These techniques and strategies are good examples of differentiation for vocabulary teaching and learning. Students must be able to see words, hear words, read words, write words, and speak words over and over again and in several contexts in order to build their vocabulary.

4. **Select words from reading materials with which students interact.**

    Research shows that vocabulary words should come from the materials that students read. Vocabulary is best learned in context. According to Fischer, "Targeted words should be drawn from authentic experiences in reading and listening, where students encounter words in the context of language" (1994). Students read several texts, both fiction and non-fiction, in my classroom. From these selections, I gather lists of vocabulary words which I believe the students do not know and words which they would need to know in order to comprehend the full meaning of the passages.

Anderson and Nagy state that, "Teaching word meanings in an abstract and decontextualized manner is essentially futile and potentially misleading" (1991). Teachers should choose words that are necessary for understanding the text and words that are likely to occur in other contexts. Students should try to infer new word meanings from context where possible, although vocabulary learning is more than just figuring out the meaning of words from context. High-interest context will engage students as they learn new vocabulary. Studies have shown that when students read materials that interest them, they become active readers and learning vocabulary becomes more meaningful and useful for them.

Reading materials containing vocabulary words for study should match students' reading levels. Students feel a sense of accomplishment when they are required to read text at their independent reading levels. Some of the reading passages I use in my classroom come from the following curriculums: *Daily Comprehension* (non-fiction) and *Spectrum* (realistic fiction). Students use various teacher-created vocabulary worksheets to interact with the vocabulary words they learn. Teachers need, therefore, to explicitly teach words which are related to the content of the reading materials.

5. **Offer time for self-selection of reading materials in print-rich learning environments.**

Research also shows the importance of teachers designing lessons to allot enough time for students to read in school. They should also assign reading outside of school. "Time spent reading, both inside and outside of school, is essential to developing vocabulary," says Stahl and Fairbanks, (1986) and Nagy, Herman, and Anderson, (1985). Nagy, Herman, and Anderson further state, "Large scale vocabulary growth results when there is a sufficient volume of wide reading" (1985). Squires affirms that "Reading many different types of material has benefits because it enables students to see words in a variety of contexts. The meanings of these words are then more easily accessible during future reading ..." and "... Both students with low- and high-level literacy skills benefit from time spent reading; vocabulary is learned from context, and comprehension is improved if the difficulty of the material presented is appropriate to the current reading level (1995). According to Nagy and his colleagues, "K-12 students will encounter about 85,000 words in print" (Marzano, *et al.* 2001).

To help students benefit from wide-scale reading, teachers must make their classrooms print-rich where students can encounter more and more vocabulary words. I use grant money to purchase high-interest books with low readability for my students. Students select the books they want to read. The first ten or fifteen minutes of class is designated to silent reading. It is amazing to see how much the students' vocabulary improves by the end of the semester! Their active vocabulary (both oral and written) reflects the benefits of learning in a print-rich environment. High-interest context will motivate and engage students as they learn new vocabulary. I have noticed that when students read materials that interest them, they become active readers and learning vocabulary becomes more meaningful and useful for them. If learners are to be optimally rounded in understanding the world, each educator must make a concerted effort to develop extensive vocabulary instruction programs.

6. **Make learning vocabulary fun by incorporating games and other fun activities.**

Learning vocabulary does not have to be a burden. Teachers can make vocabulary instruction fun and engaging for their students. Learning vocabulary through games is one of the best techniques for teaching vocabulary to both young and older learners. Games do offer activities that cater to students' sensory modalities (visual, auditory, kinesthetic). We live in a rather interactive age, and students just love to manipulate visual images. Learning vocabulary through game is fun and addictive. Using games is a beneficial way to incorporate technology into learning. Besides the websites for computer games (which I have listed in the appendix), sometimes I use *Vocabulary Cartoon* as a way of capturing students' interest in becoming word conscious and to help them develop a love of words when teaching them vocabulary. These fun cartoons aid in the memorization of words and their meanings.

The vocabulary cartoon activities provide various contexts that expose students to the word. The cartoon page includes the word, the sound spelling of the pronunciation of the word, a funny, catchy mnemonic for remembering the word, a humorous picture with caption that demonstrates the meaning of the word, and three sentences that show how the word could be used. I design a specific worksheet that matches each section of the cartoon page for students to use for direct interaction with each word they study. Below is brief explanation of the activities.

During the vocabulary unit, when students enter the room, the *Vocabulary Cartoon* page is already on the overhead projector. Each student gets a vocabulary sheet on which they will do several things with the word. They will: copy the word, read the word, determine or guess the word parts (prefix, suffix, base word, root word), study spelling patterns and chunk into morphemes (smallest unit of meaning), write the meaning of each word part, determine the part of speech and the meaning of the word based on all the sections of the cartoon page. They will consult with the instructor to see if their guess was correct. If it is correct, they will proceed to get the dictionary meaning, use a thesaurus to find a synonym, use the word in a sentence, and draw a picture related to their sentence.

Students seem to learn and remember key vocabulary better when they can associate new words with mnemonics. The vocabulary cartoon incorporates mnemonics and has context that suits students' readability levels, appeals to their interests and age group, and includes pictures, too! Using the *Vocabulary Cartoon* technique is probably the most motivating activity to get reluctant learners hooked on learning vocabulary.

7. **Assess students' vocabulary development both formally and informally.**

Assessment of vocabulary is important and should be done before the lesson, during the lesson, and after the lesson. During the lesson, there are several progress-monitoring tools for teachers to use in assessing vocabulary development. Students can take a formal quiz or test as an after-the-lesson assessment. According to Johnson, "Vocabulary knowledge increases when new words are linked to students' prior knowledge" (1981). Knowledge Rating Scales (KRS) is a chart used as a pre-reading tool to assess student's background knowledge of the vocabulary words they are about to learn. I use Knowledge Rating Scales to assess students' prior knowledge of the words on the weekly list of vocabulary words.

There are several versions of the KRS chart, so teachers can use the same tool, but with various strategies. The basic chart has about four or five columns, and the vocabulary words are written in the left column. The other columns have rating scales concerning each word, such as *know the word well, heard of it, never seen it,* etc. Students are required to check the column that applies to each word. If they check that they know the word, they will orally or in writing express the meaning of the word. This activity gives the teacher a wealth of information before she/he begins explicit instruction on the vocabulary words. Several samples of Knowledge Rating Scales can be found on the website of the National Behaviour Support service (see bibliography).

• • •

Section 4: Appendix

Websites for vocabulary and games:
1. www.freerice.com
2. www.vocabulary.co.il
3. http://www.enhancemyvocabulary.com/
4. EnglishClub.com
5. Yourdictionary.com

Websites for interest:
1. Iconn.org
2. www.adlit.org

Lexile Readability website
The Lexile Readability Index is a guide to help teachers select appropriate reading materials for students based on the students' reading levels and the readability level of the text.

Directions:
- www.Lexile.com
- Educators
- Tools
- Lexile Power Vocabulary
- Book Search (tab at upper right)
- Find a book with Lexile
- Find a book
- Put in Lexile measure
- Continue Interest
- Show me books

- Look it up (if you want to)

The Lexile Framework (levels) for Reading

First – Second Grade ----------------- 300-500
Third Grade---------------------------- 500-700
Fourth Grade-------------------------- 600-800
Fifth Grade---------------------------- 800-900
Sixth Grade---------------------------- 900-1000
Seventh Grade------------------------- 950-1030
Eighth Grade-------------------------- 1000-1100
Ninth Grade--------------------------- 1030-1120
Tenth Grade--------------------------- 1100-1200
Eleventh Grade---------------------- 1120-1210
Twelfth Grade------------------------ 1210-1300
College and Beyond------------------ 1240-1700

• • •

Section 5: Glossary of Vocabulary Terms

Affixes - suffixes and prefixes
Base Word - a plain English word. Ex: govern in government

Derivative - a base word plus a suffix

Suffix - a letter or group of letters added to the end of a base word; morphemes or units of meaning

Consonant Suffix - a suffix that begins with a consonant

Vowel Suffix - a suffix that begins with a vowel

Vocabulary - words used by a particular people or a group of persons

Lexile - a framework for reading that helps to determine if a book is too easy, too difficult, or just right for a reader

Morpheme - any of the minimal grammatical units of a language

Grapheme - a minimal unit of a writing system

Phoneme - basic distinctive unit of sound

Root word – part of a word that remains after any suffixes and/or prefixes have been removed. Root words cannot stand on their own as a word. Ex: vis in visible

Lexeme - a lexical unit

Lexicology - the study of the formation and use of words

Lexicography - the writing editing or the compiling of dictionaries

Lexicographer - a writer or editor or compiler of a dictionary

Lexical Meaning - the meaning of a base morpheme

Lexicalize - to convert into a Lexical item using the suffix-ism as the noun ism   -

Lexical - of or pertaining to the words or vocabulary of a language

• • •

Section 6: Bibliography

Allen, Janet. *Words, Words, Words: Teaching Vocabulary in Grades 4-12.* Maine: Stenhouse Publishers, 1999.

Bear, Donald, R., Invernizzi., Marcia, Templeton, Shane., and Johnston, Francine. *Words Their Way: Word Study for Phonics, Vocabulary, and Spelling Instruction.* Ohio: Pearson Education, Inc., 2004.

Biemiller, Andrew. "Teaching Vocabulary: Early, direct, and sequential" [Online] Available <http://www.aft.org/pubs-reports/american_educator/spring2001/vocab.html>, 2001.

Ivy Rose 2003. "Biology: Prefixes and Suffixes" [Online] Available http://www.ivy-rose.co.uk/Biology/Biology_Prefixes_and_suffixes.php

Brainy Quote. [Online] Available http://www.brainy quote. com/
quotes/keywords/vocabulary.html#jj42gIV3DUjVRp6X.99

Connecticut State Department of Education. *Beyond the Blueprint:
Literacy in Grades 4-12 and Across the Content Areas.*
Connecticut: Bureau of Curriculum and Instruction, 2007.

English Club. [Online] Available http://www.englishclub.com/
vocabulary/index.htm, 1997-2012

Feldman, Kevin, and Kinsella, Kate. "Narrowing the Language
Gap: The Case for the Explicit Vocabulary Instruction." Read
About. Scholastic Professional Paper. 2005.

Ganske, Kathy. *Word Journeys: Assessment-Guided Phonics, Spelling,
and Vocabulary Instruction.* New York: The Guilford press,
2000.

Marzano, Robert, J., Pickering, Debra, J. & Pollock, Jane, E.
*Classroom Instruction that Works: Research-Based Strategies for
Increasing Student Achievement.* Ohio: Pearson, 2001.

National Behaviour Support Service http://www.nbss.ie/sites/
default/files/publications/vocabulary_rating_comprehension_
strategy_ 0.pdf

National Reading Panel. (2001). *About the NRP - Charge.* Retrieved
November 27, 2012, from
http://www. nationalreadingpanel.org/NRPAbout/
Charge.htm.

Nym, Cinny. "Vocabulary" [Online] Available
www.vocabulary.com/archive.html>, 17 November 2007.

Random House. Webster's Unabridged Dictionary. New York,
2001.

Sonoma County Office of Education.
"Vocabulary/Comprehension" [Online] Available
http://www. scoe.org/content.php?PageId=169>, 2003.

The Lexile Framework for Reading. "Lexile Power Vocabulary" [Online] Available <http://www.lexile.com/DesktopDefault. aspx?view=ed&tabindex=2&tabid=16&tabpageid>

The Lexile Framework for Reading. "Find a Book with Lexiles" [Online] Available www.lexile.com/findabook/ hatarelexiles.aspx>,

Webster's Unabridged Dictionary. Random House, Inc. NY. 2001

Student Books:

These are samples of books I use in the classroom. Various levels of these books can be adapted for different grade levels.

Billins, Henry, and Melissa. *In the Spotlight.* Ohio: Glencoe/McGraw-Hill, 2007.

Burchers, Sam, Max, and Bryan. *Vocabulary Cartoons: Kids Learn a Word a Minute and Never Forget It.* Florida: New Monic Books, 1998.

Fry, Edward B. *Vocabulary Drills.* Illinois: Jamestown Publishers, 2000.

Fry, Edward B. *Reading Drills.* Illinois: Jamestown Publishers, 2000.

Pavlik, Robert, and Ramsey, Richard, G. *Reading & Writing Source Book.* Massachusetts: Houghton Mifflin Company, 2000.

• • •

CORINNE THOMPSON is an expert reading consultant, an enthusiastic reading teacher, and an amazing special education teacher. She has over ten years experience teaching reading, writing, and executive functioning skills at the elementary, secondary and tertiary levels.

She successfully completed degrees in the following areas: Diploma - Elementary Education, Mico Teachers' College, Jamaica W. I.; B.A. - Sociology/Elementary Education, Lehman

College, Bronx, NY; M.S.- Reading, Lehman College, Bronx, NY; M.S., Special Education, Southern Connecticut State University; and Sixth Year Professional Degree, Southern Connecticut State University.

She currently holds the following certifications: Remedial Reading & Remedial Language Arts, Grades 1-12 (102); Comprehensive special Education, Grades K-12 (165); Elementary, Grades K-6 (005); Reading Consultant Certification, Grades K-12 (097).

Contact her by email at: corinnethompson@sbcglobal.net.

EFFECTIVE INSTRUCTIONAL PRACTICES

• • • Michelle Golla-Sralik • • •

WHEN I THINK OF instructional practices that will work in any classroom, several things come to mind: instilling a desire to want to learn more about the subject matter; building confidence in the students to want to succeed; providing students with opportunities to develop a deeper understanding of the subject matter through practice, reasoning, problem solving and exploration; and finally, including integrated activities accessible to all—differentiation for students to move from easier to hard levels, which ensures that every student will succeed and love to learn.

Can anyone go into a classroom and wave a magic wand to make this happen? It is achievable, but what steps need to be taken to get there? A starting point is being educated and experienced in educational and classroom best practices. What educational best practices make a teacher become more effective? Knowing the basic ones will be a jump-start. Of course, there is so much to learn, but understanding the importance of research-based strategies on what works and what doesn't, what resources can be used to support you, and what professional development opportunities can be taken to get you there will move you in the right direction.

Genuine reformers are recognizing that schools aren't failing due to administrative reasons, lack of resources, shortage of supports in the classroom, or large class sizes. This contributes to the system coming undone, but researchers have concluded that the root cause is ineffective teachers. Therefore, one must get to the heart of actual day-to-day teaching. The biggest concern has been whether teachers are adequately prepared to step into a classroom and deal with the plethora of "must dos," especially knowing the content and how to teach it.

Following the standards and frameworks for all content areas in a best practices paradigm, the demand is to have more progressive, experiential, collaborative, student-centered, cognitive and critical thinking, and hands-on and self-sponsored activities for students to move forward in their learning. Most teachers rating exemplary will claim that the aforementioned took years to master, but it is food for thought to move one forward to be an effective teacher. These characteristics of effective instructional practices have been something explored by the finest educators and proven to work!

Of course, much work needs to be done on a daily basis to refine instruction. It is about being a learner, as if you were a student seeking opportunities to grow, extend, fine-tune, and be intentional. If you dare to teach, you must dare to learn to improve your practices.

Some first steps to improve your best practices are to consult the experts through obtaining resources on best practices for teaching and learning in your school (See Marzano's *Classroom Instruction That Works*) and take advantage of professional development opportunities offered by your district and/or educational organizations across the state or at your school. This can be found on your district website, through the Department of Education, or your teachers' union. Observe effective classrooms, either by watching video clips or visiting classrooms that run the gambit of having low to high performing students in the class, students in an urban, suburban, or rural setting, and make it a point to visit a class filled with a diverse student-body (ELL, SPED, ED, FRL, GT, HGT, AN), which can be one of the best ways to modify your practices to meet the needs of all. In addition, to move ahead in your practice, request a mentor teacher who has been recognized as being skilled in instructional planning, has strong classroom and organization and management, has fluency with multiple methods of delivering instruction, uses multiple methods for student assessment, demonstrates success in their work as classroom teachers, articulates their practice, and reflects on their own practice. These types of teachers are usually the teacher leaders in the building who listen skillfully, communicate effectively, can diagnose the needs of struggling teachers, and are willing to align support to identified needs of teachers (Killion, J. Harrison, C. 2006).

The following Best Practices or Measures of Effective Teaching and Instruction, or some other name that has been and still is being tested and refined in classrooms, is based on sound learning theory and has helped many educational analysts across the country identify the characteristics and practices to improve effective teaching. Using research from years past to present day, it all boils down to the following, which has been borrowed from many.

First Days

To be effective in one's instructional practices, taking the necessary steps prior to the school year starting is a key to success in the classroom and is linked to academic achievement for the students. Those first days will either make or break you. Ask yourself the following questions. What are the things that need to be in place at the beginning of the year? How do I build relationships with the students to build their trust and respect? If an observer or evaluator walks into the classroom, what are the most important items that need to be seen to reflect what the students are and will be learning? What needs to be taught, and how will I teach it? How will learning be maximized for all students? How does one focus strictly on the interaction between the students and teachers and not on zealous reform? How do I enhance student achievement?

Douglas Brooks, author of *First Day of School Educational Leadership*, pp. 76-78, observed a group of ineffective and effective teachers. The ineffective teachers started their first days with a fun activity, but chased kids around all year. The effective ones spent time organizing their rooms so students can learn, grow, and become productive citizens. It is all about learning. Those first days are about laying the ground rules, building strong relationships by learning students' names, interests, learning styles and habits, but foremost, putting into place positive expectations for student success. Your expectations will influence students' achievement in and out of the classroom and determine what is and isn't expected to happen every day. Once these expectations are in place, students will trust that you believe they are capable of growing to their fullest potential, that you are the key to their success, and that the classroom is intentionally inviting for all. Adapted from Harry Wong's *The First Days of School.*

Classroom Management

In order to be effective with instruction, the teacher needs to be a good classroom manager. It is important to organize a well-managed classroom to support learning in a task-oriented environment. Arrange your classroom for easy movement to maximize learning and minimize behaviors. Put into place a discipline plan for your year to run smoothly. Set up and teach procedures and routines to maintain structure and order—which is students thrive on. Present rules in a clear and precise way, so all students know the classroom boundaries and understand the consequences that will be enforced and rewards that will be given. Set limits, usually five rules (Be Prompt, Be Prepared, Be Positive, Be Productive, Be Polite), to tell students how far they can go. Be consistent with follow-through. Capitalize on learning by being prepared every day (even over prepare) to avoid down time, which opens opportunities for off-task behavior. When considering those off-task behaviors, discuss with your disciplinarian interventions that could be used for students who tend to sway easily. Consult with your peers on what has worked for them in the past and present. Refer to the RTI model (Response to Intervention) to improve student outcomes.

Stand firm on your demands, but communicate in both a warm and non-negotiable way to maximize student effort and mutual respect. This is central to sustaining academic engagement, especially in high-poverty schools. The stakes are high when it comes to engagement. Studies have amply demonstrated a link between positive behavior, achievement, and academic engagement, defined by Furrer and Skinner (2003) as "active, goal-directed, flexible, constructive, persistent, and focused interactions" with academic tasks (p. 149.) Teachers of this nature tend to be viewed as harsh. Instead, they have class control and high expectations of the students that have resulted in positive outcomes – academic achievement.

Using a rich base of research on effective classroom techniques to help manage the classroom is most critical to have in place for success to occur in the classroom. It doesn't take someone who is a master teacher in educational practices and the subject matter to achieve this. Anything is possible for someone who is willing to take on the challenge and endure the complexity of change.

Lesson Mastery

Create lessons for student mastery that are meaningful, have impact, are intentional, and invite engagement. If the students aren't learning, you've failed them. When planning, be deliberate with the main purpose in mind: seeking academic excellence for your students.

Pay special attention to designing lessons that vary in the level of cognitive demand to support the needs of all learners. Students need to be moving from the lower level, such as memorization, to midlevel, such as following procedures without connections, to higher levels of thinking. Provide tasks that will challenge the students to delve deeper into understanding the concepts and ideas. This can include representing the material in multiple ways for students to access the material and develop meaning. Require students to explore and understand the nature of the concepts, processes, or relationships and analyze and examine the task for strategies to find solutions or to address the issues.

Demand self-monitoring of one's own cognitive processes and growth by setting long- and short-term goals, but make yourself accountable to do so, as well. As a result, students are more likely to buy into it. Progress monitoring students' growth, as well using multiple assessments, is a way to assess a child's academic performance and evaluate the effectiveness of instruction. In addition, having students set short- and long-term goals will encourage them to establish a direction and own their learning. Teachers can utilize students' data to drive planning and instruction.

Think about the content and practices that you hope the students will learn from their work on the lesson(s). Build on what you have available when planning the lessons. If you have a particular set of language items you want to teach, a basic lesson outline, and lots of different activities, then planning the lesson is fun. If you lack any of those three things, lesson planning can be very frustrating. Questions like, what should I teach, what should I do first, and how should I teach it can plague you every time. Keep it fun and rewarding for the students, or it will end up being the most frustrating experience you can imagine (Krause, 2000).

Once this is mapped, determine the learning objective. Learning goals need to be specific, measureable, and attainable, but adaptable in order for the students to know exactly what is expected of them, what will be taught, and what needs to be accomplished by the end of the lesson.

Teachers need to be culturally responsive when planning the lesson by accounting for the various ethnic backgrounds represented in the classroom and incorporate real-life applications and technology. All kids learn and respond differently to situations. Therefore, it is crucial that you are skilled in knowing how to relate to kids of all nature. Some ideas are giving assignments that are clear and concise, that require the students to be engaged and working at all times whether it be in whole group, in partners, cooperative and collaborative groups, or independently. Constantly reflecting on your practices will help you recognize your weaknesses, especially with how you respond to students from different *intellectual, social, socioeconomic, and racial backgrounds.*

Moving Forward in Your Practices

The ideas of the past, starting in the 60's, have experienced a resurgence where progressive actions in education are challenging the current educational system to shift its philosophical and political views of education and balance it with pedagogical understanding of the fundamentals of how children learn and their capabilities. This emergence is to create opportunities for children to be exposed to rigorous challenges, open to engaging in ways to experiment with the subject matter, apply those experiences to real-life situations, and take charge of their own learning. The ultimate reason for this push for change is to prepare our students to compete globally. Other countries have surpassed us in all subject areas, especially math and science. How have we failed our children to get to this point—not learning from the past models that were working at the time and moving our country forward? Teachers took steps backwards to being the sage on the stage of the 1930's, and it could be the reason for our failing schools; but with this renewal of thought, teachers don't have the lead role. Instead, the students do. The role of teachers now is to guide the students in their learning, provide a safe haven, offer choices, encourage engagement, and attend to their needs. This reemergence focuses on the ideals of the more/less model, which consists of thirteen characteristics that are the model to education (Zemelman, et al. 1998).

Student Centered- Teacher serves as facilitator to help students understand the common objectives and assist in the planning to achieve their goals;

Experiential – Active, hands-on, concrete experiences;

Holistic – The meaning of the content evolves making the lesson more purposeful;

Authentic – Real, rich, complex ideas at the heart of the lesson;

Expressive – Students employ a range of communicative ideas;

Reflective – Opportunities are provided for students to reflect on their learning;

Social – Offer classroom interactions that "scaffold" learning;

Collaborative – Cooperative-learning activities are provided to prepare students for real-world interactions;

Democratic – Students learning about what it is to be members of society;

Cognitive – Tapping into higher-order thinking to make sense of the concepts presented;

Developmental – Students going through definable and not rigid steps to problem solving;

Constructivist – Students don't just receive the content; instead they make sense of it;

Challenging – Students are exposed to a rigorous curriculum;

In the Denver Public Schools, Denver, CO, a Framework for Effective Teaching was developed and is increasingly being recognized nationally for its high-quality structure. This model, called Leading Effective Academic Practice, is an initiative and support system to provide feedback, development, coaching, and growth for the teachers in the district. Teachers and school leaders developed the frameworks, putting emphasis on the critical elements of innovation, creativity, teamwork, problem-solving, and critical thinking in order to develop the whole child, make them well-rounded learners, and prepare them for success in college and career. This model is an excellent reference tool to use to hone your professional craft and nurture your students' growth in all ways (Bosberg, Tom. 2010). Go to the DPS website for information on the LEAP model. The DPS Framework for Effective Teaching emphasizes the key expectations of teachers: Building a Positive Classroom Culture and Climate, Effective Classroom Management, Standards-Based Goals, High Impact Instructional Moves, Differentiation, Masterful Content Knowledge, and Academic Language Development and 21st Century Skills. Using the tool plays a pivotal part in deepening the knowledge of teachers in order for them to be more effective – something recommended for refining and improving your skills.

In conclusion, this is the most critical time in our country, and our role is the most important, with a focus on how we develop and promote the highest quality teaching in all our classrooms – teaching that reaches and enriches the whole child and helps our kids develop the creative, critical, higher-order thinking skills that all of them need to succeed in the community and in the workforce. This calls for teachers who are thought provoking, caring, organized, tolerant, flexible, sensitive, motivated, excited, and efficient about learning. If you don't possess these qualities—wear the various hats—maybe, maybe this isn't the career for you. It is about being effective in our instructional practices to ensure student achievement and continual academic progress.

Each child is living the only life he has – the only one he will ever have. The least we can do is not diminish it. --- Bill Page.

• • •

Works Cited

Krause, Aleda. 2000. *Planning a Lesson for Children*. Kids World

Wrightslaw. 2001. *The Importance of Progress Monitoring*. www.writghtslaw.com/nltr/11/nl.1206.htm.

Denver Public Schools. (2012). *Planning a Lesson*. Standards Institute.

Stein, M. K., Smith, M. S., Henningsen, M. A., & Silver, E. A. (2000). *Implementing standards- based mathematics instruction: A casebook for professional development*. New York: Teachers College Press.

National Council Teachers of Mathematics. (1991). *Professional Standards for Teaching Mathematics*.

Zemelman, Steven, Daniels, H. & Hyde, A. (1998).*Best Practice: New Standards for Teaching and Learning in America's Schools*. Heinman, Portsmouth, NH.

National Commission on Excellence in Education. (1985). *A Nation at Risk: The Imperative for Educational Reform*. Washington, DC.

Hirsh, E.D. (1996). *The Schools We Need and Why We Don't Have Them*. New York: Doubleday.

Hindley, Joanne. (1996) *In the Company of Children*. York, ME: Stenhouse Publishers.

Brooks, Douglas. (1985). *"First Day of School."* Educational Leadership, pp. 76-78.

"It Takes More Than Standards" (Editorial). (1996). New York Times. (6, December); 22.

Kendall, John S., and Robert Marzano. (1996). *Content Knowledge: A Compendium of Standards and Benchmarks for K-12 Education*. Aurora, CO: Mid-Continent Regional Educational Laboratory.

Marzano, Robert J., Pickering, Debra, Pollock, Jane E. (2001). *Classroom Instruction That Works: Research-Based Strategies For Increasing Student Achievement*. McRel.

Wong, Harry K. & Rosemary T. Wong. (1998). *The First Days of School: How to be an Effective Teacher.* Harry Wong Publications.

Killion, J. Harrison, C. (2006). *Taking the Lead: New Roles for Coaches and Teacher Leaders.* National Staff Development Council, in press. Oxford, OH

Furrer, C. J., Skinner, E. A., & Pitzer, J. R. (in press).*The Influence of Teacher and Peer Relationships on Students' Classroom Engagement and Everyday Resilience.* In D.J. Shernoff & J. Bempechat (Eds.), *National Society for the Study of Education Yearbook: Engaging Youth in Schools: Empirically-based Models to Guide Future Innovations.*

Bosberg, Tom. (2011). *LEAP Model.* Denver Public Schools.www.dpsk12.org.

Leading Effective Academic Practice, LEAP. (2010). Denver Public Schools. Denver, CO. www.dpsk12.org.

ENGAGEMENT STRATEGIES THAT IMPROVE STUDENT PARTICIPATION

• • • Elizabeth Nordyke • • •

I WILL NEVER FORGET visiting classrooms during my first year as a principal and noticing what a great disparity there was in teacher lessons. In one room, I saw the apathy of the students. Some were chatting, a boy was busily crafting a paper airplane in his desk, and a girl was getting a drink of water, while another boy searched his backpack for some markers. With her back to the class, Mrs. S. was lecturing and writing on the board, doing all the work while no one was paying attention. She was so busy speaking and writing she had no idea that her students were entertaining themselves, instead of learning. When she turned around, they dutifully acted like they were paying attention, and then Mrs. S. finished with the question, "Do you understand?" None of the students responded to her question. She did not really expect anyone to answer, but told the students to get out their books. They started an assignment, and everyone was confused. Multiple hands were raised and comments made, such as, "I don't get it!" With that lesson typical of her teaching style, is it any wonder that Mrs. S. displayed angst when her student scores came in lower than other colleagues on the annual standardized tests?

In the room next door, Mr. V. created an entirely different atmosphere. He was projecting and working problems on the board. The students' attention was riveted toward the teacher and their task. Every student had a whiteboard at their desk, which they used to alternate doing problems with Mr. V. Student answers were immediately checked and corrected as Mr. V.

called on different students to respond. The room was alive with passion and activity. Students were working harder than Mr. V. as he checked for understanding, with observable data leading to reteaching, as necessary. As expected with their level of understanding, the students were successful. Each year in May, when the standardized tests were given, Mr. V. was thrilled to have his students score at the advanced level!

I will never forget the contrast as I set out to give post-observation feedback to teachers with such different styles of instruction. I needed to work differently with each teacher. I worked with Mrs. S. to build her level of student engagement, as it is the hallmark of an exceptional teacher and is created when the teacher asks the students to do something. The teacher who masters engaging his or her students is the teacher who retains zest and passion for his or her entire career. Mr. V. is a 20year veteran teacher, and he exudes enthusiasm and his students demonstrate the greatest level of academic success. Student and teacher are rewarded with excitement for learning and unparalleled achievement.

As a 25-year elementary school principal, I have observed hundreds of classrooms. Many of the students are English learners and are from low socioeconomic backgrounds. Significant home issues such as poverty, crime, gang involvement, parents working two or three jobs, and chronic attendance issues serve as challenges for teachers. The challenge to teach with academic rigor at grade level standards can best be done with student engagement strategies. In my last school, my staff and I achieved API (Academic Performance Index) growth from 644 to 839 on the California Standards Test (CST). Student engagement strategies were a key component of the extraordinary gains. Every classroom teacher became skilled at implementing routine practices throughout the day. As a principal, my observations and feedback always spoke to engagement. I challenged teachers to push for more and more engagement and rigor. As these strategies were implemented school wide, academic learning increased and the students had more fun. The parents became more supportive, and discipline issues were minimal.

Teachers spend significant time planning and preparing lessons, but it is the delivery and engagement during the lesson that determines the student outcomes. Even though Mrs. S. worked hard, spending hours writing perfect lesson plans and demonstrating a caring spirit, she did not use engagement strategies, and all of her work fell on deaf ears.

What is engagement? Eric Jensen (2009) defines engagement as, "a strategy that gets students to participate emotionally, cognitively, or behaviorally." The goal of the teacher is to do all three.

Engagement strategies are needed to maximize learning. The days of lecture and worksheets are outdated and ineffective. Not only does the lecture and fill-in-the-blank mode turn off students, but children who are continuing to learn English are especially vulnerable. The students are desperate for visuals, connections, explanations, and time to process and show their work. Implementing the strategies outlined below allows this to be accomplished. It is imperative that each taught lesson has a clearly defined objective, a teaching model and guided practice format that concludes with determining what was learned. John Hollingsworth(2009) describes "Explicit Direct Instruction" and the gift of excellent first teaching. This involves incorporating the following strategies into the lesson plan to increase student mastery.

Pair Share

Pair share is one of the easiest and most powerful strategies, if done correctly. The process must be taught carefully, as follows. After teaching for about 5 to 10 minutes, the students do partner talk, where there are the two partners, often called elbow partners. They can be named A, B partners or clever names that appeal to students based on age, such as peanut butter and jelly for primary and sports teams for older students. Mrs. M. asks a question and has A tell B their answer. Then B can tell A his response. She then gives a previously taught signal to have students stop sharing and have all eyes on her. She then calls on a non-volunteer student to share what his partner said, clarifying as needed. The beauty of this strategy is that all students are participating. When properly trained and knowing that Mrs. M. will require a response, the students stay focused and everyone is learning together. Pair-share is most effective when behavioral expectations are clear and the pacing is fast.

Whiteboards

All students have a whiteboard and a marker. This can be a small white chalkboard, lined or unlined. A less expensive option is a white paper in a laminate sheet from which the marker can be erased. The markers can be any non-permanent marker, such as Dry Erase. Students may use a small eraser or an old sock from home. As a principal, I provide these materials to all classes, so this strategy will be used daily. Mr. J. models a problem and then has the students do a problem on the whiteboard. Upon hearing his signal, the students hold up their work for Mr. J. to give feedback in real time. Mistakes and misunderstandings are addressed before poor practice becomes permanent. Whiteboards are effective because all students are held accountable and all are participating.

Responders

Many classrooms have Smartboards and student responders. Lessons incorporate questions and checking for understanding as the lesson is progressing. Students respond, and their answers immediately are shown in a circle graph, with the percentage of students understanding the concept reflected in the instantaneous data. Reteaching can occur in the moment, rather than waiting for a chapter test at the end of the week. Smartboards reflect which students are answering first and how long it takes for each student to answer. Mrs. T. is watching which students will be last to respond, knowing that those students may be having trouble understanding. Mrs. T. checks on any student that made an error, and she can ask the student why an answer was selected and clarify misconceptions. Walking through classrooms, I really smile as the students shout with joy when the entire class demonstrates correct answers. Content knowledge is a requirement that precedes the Common Core Standards requiring a product or a process. The thinking process is examined as a student shares why and how he selected an answer. Student demonstration and interaction with the Smartboard heightens the academic achievement. The year our school began teaching with Smartboards, our API went up an additional 35 points. I believe the visual impact of the teaching, with the interaction and the student data outcomes, provided a motivation and an opportunity for checking for understanding in the moment.

Higher-Level Thinking /Bloom's Taxonomy

In 2001, one of Benjamin Bloom's students revised the hierarchy of educational objectives. Bloom's Taxonomy allows teachers to instruct students at cognitive levels. Knowledge/Remembering/Comprehending/Understanding Application/Applying Synthesis and Evaluation are ways of demonstrating student knowledge. Evaluating and Creating can be used to increase complexity. Students of all ages can be asked questions from the different levels. The student learning can be differentiated by the levels and complexity of the questions asked.

Manipulatives

Fraction pieces, place value charts, money, clocks, and other hands-on manipulatives allow students to accomplish tasks successfully. They are actively participating and demonstrating their knowledge. They must be engaged since they are actively moving pieces. Students show what they know and are not passive listeners to a lecture. As a long-time principal doing observations and evaluations, the difference between a primary teacher that uses manipulatives and one that does not is evident. The student scores are different. The feeling tone is different. The use of manipulatives requires processing by the students. They are engaged and focused while using manipulatives. The teacher can see which student does not understand. Manipulatives are fun, and all students do better on abstract problems after having had a chance to actually demonstrate conceptual knowledge. In my experience, classrooms with the manipulatives have better outcomes and higher academic achievement based on our yearly statewide test (CST). Last year, my school's second-grade students had the highest scores in math for our entire district on the CST (76% proficient or advanced). Undoubtedly, the teachers' regular use of manipulatives and other engagement strategies outlined in this chapter led to the academic success.

Stand and Deliver

How often does one child answer a question in one word, using a timid, quiet voice, while 29 others sit, unable to hear? Many of my teachers ask their students to stand and respond. The response is given in a firm voice and in a complete sentence, using academic vocabulary. After answering the question or giving his response, he sits. This stand and then sit is done quickly and daily. Class members value all student responses, and all students can hear. This process creates a classroom environment where what students have to say to each other is of importance. I especially enjoy watching kindergarten and first-grade students share this way and smile as their class members appreciate what they have to say. Sometimes young children will be so proud for others to speak and answer that the little students applaud. This strategy can also be used with the non-volunteer strategy for maximum accountability.

Choral Reading

In many classrooms, students are asked to chorally read out of the text. For this to be meaningful for all students, all must read. They may use their two pointer fingers to frame the sentence, moving down the page as the selection is read. The teacher can vary the reading by calling on table groups, teams, students wearing red, boys, girls, brunettes, etc. Students will be ready and alert, and the teacher can assist or clarify as needed during the choral read. Choral reading is important for students to read grade-level material that is at a higher level than their independent reading level. Teachers can also ask questions and require students to find information in the text and frame it with their fingers. I enjoy watching teachers who have perfected this skill. The reading, questions, and vocabulary are at grade level. All students can access the text in this method.

Calling on Non-Volunteers

Students become more engaged when they are aware that they can be called on at any moment. The key is to train students not to raise their hands in class. This goes against standard procedure. When a teacher is able to train the students not to raise their hands, the three or four that answer "right" every time will not be the only voices heard. To randomly call on students, the teacher can use sticks with students' names or numbers on them. A deck of playing cards with student names or numbers can be easily held in your hand. The "random caller" on the Smartboard will also select a student in game show fashion. Regardless of the technique used, the unpredictability of being called on creates the need for unwavering student engagement.

The above strategies are but a few of many that can make lessons engaging and more memorable. When the level of student engagement is higher, the level of student learning is also higher. A child is, indeed, fortunate when instructed by a masterful teacher who embraces the engagement strategies. In the long run, our students retain information longer because they had an opportunity to be engaged with the learning objective.

There are endless instructional strategies that educators can master. The use of these strategies will make learning or achievement of an educational goal easier, more rapid, and more predictably successful for a student. As a principal, I see the importance of my role in helping teachers develop and use engagement strategies. The school becomes a vital learning environment where everyone benefits.

• • •

ELIZABETH NORDYKE lives in Orange County, California, and has been a primary teacher, a reading teacher, staff developer, and a principal. She is a turnaround specialist and has opened a new school and served at underperforming schools to increase their academic achievement. She speaks at various conferences, and her schools have won the California Distinguished School and Title One Achieving Schools Awards. She was the Administrator of the Year in her district.

BRAIN-COMPATIBLE PROCESSING STRATEGIES

• • • Annette Jones • • •

IT HAS HAPPENED TO all of us. We've prepared and taught a lesson which we thought was relevant and interesting, yet the key concepts were not retained by our students. Why? In analyzing brain functions, scientists have found that when information is introduced into the brain, it is either filed or discarded (Gregory & Parry, Designing Brain-Compatible Learning, 2006). The brain first tries to file information by attaching it to existing knowledge. If the information cannot be attached to existing knowledge, then the brain must construct meaning from the information, creating multiple pathways with which to retrieve it. Information that has not undergone one of those two processes is discarded and forgotten. To ensure that new information is filed and retained, students need time in which to process it.

Furthermore, research shows that the average student can effectively concentrate on one task for a number of minutes equal to their age, plus or minus two minutes (Armstrong, 2008). For example, eight year olds can focus for an average of six to ten minutes. It is imperative, therefore, for educators to pause within that time framework and allow students to process the information. These processing breaks need not be long, nor do they need to be graded. They do, however, need to engage all the students. This chapter will provide you with a variety of ways to allow the students time to process information and thus retain it.

Processing Strategies for the Whole Group Setting

1. **Whip Around**

   After 10 to 15 minutes of instruction, "whip" around the classroom, getting quick responses to questions regarding the key concepts just introduced. The process should be rapid, focusing on recent information. Students should use their notes and books to help them. You may choose to only question the number of students needed to review the concepts or repeat questions until everyone has been questioned. If you choose to limit the questions, be sure to begin your next whip where you left off. I usually repeat questions so all students are included and not allowed to "check out." To incorporate some movement into the class, I have had the students form a circle when we do this activity.

2. **Parking Lot**

   During a unit of study, have students write any questions or observations they may have about the topic on a sticky-note. The sticky-notes should be "parked" on a poster, which is labeled Parking Lot. At the end of the class, pull the sticky-notes off the parking lot and allow the class as a whole to discuss each question or observation, clarifying where needed.

3. **Two-Column Notes**

   Students divide a piece of notebook paper into two columns, with the left column take up about 1/3 of the paper and the right column 2/3 of the paper. Label the left column "Main Idea" and the right column "Detail." As students read a passage either independently or with a partner, have them enter information into the correct column. Model creating notes using bullet points, phrases, key concepts, and vocabulary in the left column and details, pictures, connections, reactions, questions and memory hints in the right column. Also model how the notes can be used as a study guide by covering the right column, then using the main ideas in the left column, try to explain and expand upon the concepts. Students may check themselves by uncovering the details. This strategy can also be used for conclusion/support, hypothesis/evidence, or problem/ solution notes.

Figure 1   **Two-Column Notes**
Photosynthesis

Main Idea	Detail
Definition	Process by which plants produce glucose or food
Materials	Sunlight, CO_2, H_2O
Formula	Light energy + carbon dioxide + water $\rightarrow$ glucose + water + oxygen $6\ CO_2 + 12\ H_2O \rightarrow C_6H_{12}O_6 + 6\ O_2 + 6\ H_2O$
Diagram	
	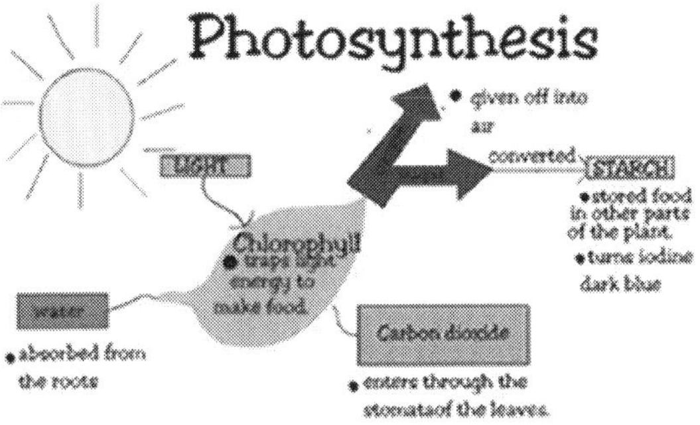 (Bixby, 2003)

4. **Give One – Get One**
   On a large (4x6) index card:
   - Write three things you learned or found interesting about the brain compatible research
   - Draw a line under the third item
   - Meet with a partner
   - Share your items

- Write down one item that your buddy had that you found interesting, never thought about, or agreed with.

I usually have students switch partners two or three times to share information.

Processing Strategies for Small Groups

1. **Read and Say Something**
   Have students read a selection silently, then turn to their partner and say anything related to the selection. Conversations will center around the meaning of the passage. You may instruct students to create a short written summary or a question or area in which they are confused and then have a whole class discussion.

2. **Picture Notes**
   Students should read an assignment, either independently, in small groups, or as a class. Organize the students into small groups. Each group gets a large piece of paper and markers. As a group, the students are to:
   - Identify the main ideas in the reading.

   - Represent the main ideas and their interconnections on the paper. Using pictures or words – I usually limit the number of words allowed to encourage the use of graphics.
   - Share their picture notes with the class.

   This activity encourages discussion as the groups identify the main ideas and how to represent them. Students actively process the information and are able to defend their choice of pictures, enabling the teacher to analyze their level of understanding of the concepts.

3. **Mind Streaming**

Following the introduction of new information, create pairs of students. Student A will talk for one minute about the topic, while student B will listen and encourage. Then reverse the roles, with student A listening and student B talking for one minute. Students can be instructed to focus on main idea/details, how the ideas relate to each other or the Big Idea being studied. I sometimes have students write for one minute before this activity. This allows the student who needs more processing time to get his ideas organized.

4. **Conversation Circles**

Form groups of three students, labeling students A, B, and C. Ask student A to begin talking about the topic until given the signal to stop. When you give the signal to stop, student B continues with the topic, and student C begins when B is signaled to stop. Students may paraphrase or make connections during their discussion.

5. **Sticky-note Discussion**

Assign a reading passage to the class. As the students read, they are to mark sections of their reading with sticky-notes, using the following code:

- ! exclamation point = something exciting or interesting
- ? = I have a question or don't understand
- ➡ = important information

Organize the class into groups. Students take turns sharing their sticky-notes with their group. Instruct the students to share why they marked that item.

6. **Timed-Pair-Paraphrase**

After introduction of new information, organize the class into pairs. Student A will have one or two minutes to respond to a question posed by the teacher, such as, "Why are producers important to the ecosystem?" Student B will listen and then have one or two minutes to paraphrase what student A said. Ask several Bs to share what they heard with the class. Then reverse roles with student B responding to a question, such as, "What is the role of decomposers in the ecosystem?" and student A paraphrasing and sharing. This activity engages all students in the classroom. If you have students who need time to process, give the class a minute to jot some notes down before beginning.

7. **Rotation Reflection**

    Post large pieces of paper around the room on which key concepts of the unit of study have been written. Assign a small group of students to each chart. Each group should discuss the concept on their chart and write their ideas on the chart. At a signal, the groups rotate to a different chart. The new group reads and discusses what is written on the chart. They then add to or elaborate on the information. Once the groups have rotated through the charts, have each group share the information on the chart at which they are currently standing. To save on chart paper, I have laminated them and used dry erase markers or sticky-notes. This is a good activity to review information at the end of the unit.

Processing Strategies for Individuals

1. **P-M-I-S**

    At the end of the class period, have students write the following on slips of paper:

    - P – a positive aspect of the topic
    - M – a minus or negative aspect of the topic
    - I – an interesting or intriguing idea from the topic
    - S – a suggestion, question, or idea into which to dig deeper

The teacher collects these as exit slips from his classroom. These exit slips help inform the teacher the level of understanding the students have. They should not be graded.

2. **Donut**

   Have students draw a large donut shape on a piece of paper. Label the inside "I Know" and the outside "I Am Learning." Before beginning the day's lesson, have students write what they know about the topic. After 10 to 15 minutes of instruction, have students write new information in the "I Am Learning" section. This activity activates prior knowledge with the "I Know" section and gives the student time to process and reflect in the "I Am Learning" section. The papers may be collected (but not graded) so the teacher may identify level of understanding. I have students keep these in their folders to be used as a tool for review.

   Figure 2: Donut

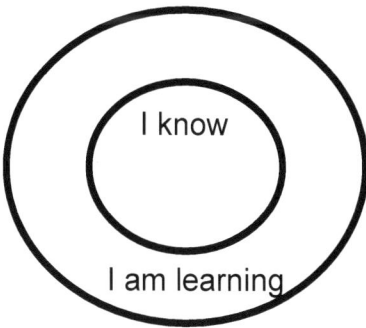

Figure 3: P-M-I-S

PMIS is an exit slip that allows students to think about what they know, have learned, and are confused about and allows the teacher to check for understanding.

P (plus, positives about the topic)
I like... I agree with... I'll remember... I'm going to use

M (minus, negatives about the topic)
   I don't like... I disagree with.... I think _____should be changed

I (intriguing, interesting about the topic)
I am still thinking about ____ because... I am not sure about _____ because...

S (suggestions or ideas for further study or questions)
Next time we can.... I wish the author would...
This would have been easier if...

3. **Instant Replay**

    Instant Replay is an exit slip that allows students to review the lesson and process the information. I use the feedback to adjust the next lesson to the needs of the class.

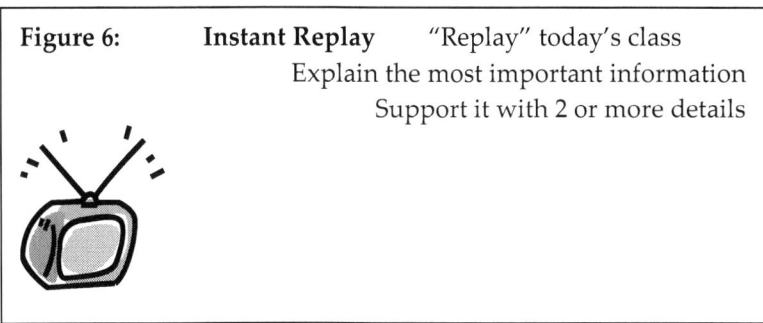

Figure 6:   **Instant Replay**   "Replay" today's class
                                    Explain the most important information
                                    Support it with 2 or more details

4. **H – Diagram**

    Create a large H on a piece of paper. Write two ideas, one on each leg of the H. On the cross bar, write characteristics or attributes that link the two ideas. I have the students do this individually so I can identify their level of understanding. At a later time, I have students share with the whole class, creating a class-size H-diagram.

Figure 4:   H – Diagram

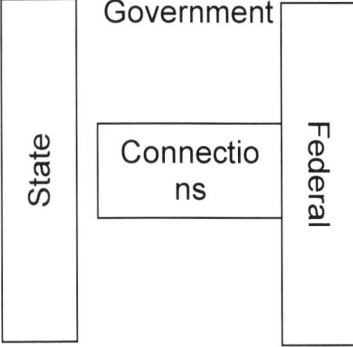

5. **Mind Mapping**

   On a piece of paper, students identify the key concepts of the lesson by using pictures or words. Lines are drawn between the sections to show how the concepts are connected. Related items can also be color coded. The map is added to as the unit progresses. I periodically collect these to identify areas that need to be reinforced. The mind map is a good tool to use for review at the end of the unit.

6. **Venn Diagram**

   Students use a Venn diagram to compare two things. Attributes of each are written in the outer circle, and attributes that both objects have are written in the overlap section. Three circles can be used to compare three things. I use this to check for understanding. At times, I have students take turns adding information to a large class-size Venn diagram.

Figure 5:   Venn Diagram

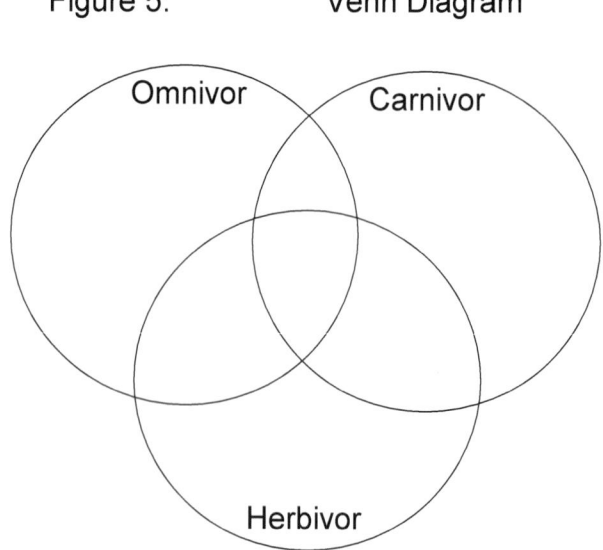

7. **Dear Teacher**

   On index cards, students write a note to the teacher. They describe their learning and ask any questions they may have. They may also ask for help with specific skills. I may respond to the students individually or to the whole class if the problem is a common one.

8. **Geometric Thinking**

   This is an exit slip that allows students to review new information, connect it to what they already know, and identify areas in which they are still confused. I use this feedback to adjust future instruction.

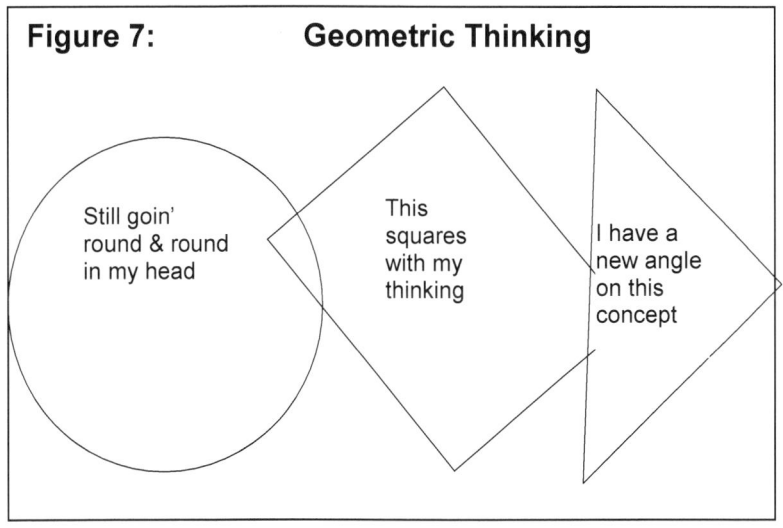

Figure 7: Geometric Thinking

Still goin' round & round in my head

This squares with my thinking

I have a new angle on this concept

Stopping every few minutes to use these strategies will help students process information. Remember, brain research shows that in order for new information to be filed into long-term memory, the brain must either connect it to existing knowledge or create a new framework into which it is filed. That takes time. These strategies help students focus on information, make connections, and clarify their thinking. Although the strategies should be used enough that students are comfortable with them, they also should be varied. If one or two strategies are used repeatedly, students will become bored with them and less engaged in their own learning. Incorporating processing strategies into my lessons has increased student engagement and metacognition. The frequent processing breaks have increased enjoyment for both my students and myself and made the class period fly.

• • •

Bibliography

Allen, L. (2008). *Differentiated Assessment & Grading.* Peterborough, NH: Crystal Springs Books.

Armstrong, S. (2008). *Teaching Smarter with the Brain in Focus.* New York: Scholastic.

Bixby, L. (2003, March 25). *Vocabulary Page.* Retrieved September 26, 2012, from Welcome to Mrs. Bixby's Web Page: http://www.labixby.com/weblinkz/vocab.html

Gregory, G. H., & Chapman, C. (2007). *Differentiated Instructional Strategies: One Size Doesn't Fit All.* Thousand Oaks, CA: Corwin Press.

Gregory, G. H., & Parry, T. (2006). *Designing Brain-Compatible Learning.* Thousand Oaks California: Corwin Press.

Hollas, B. (2007). *Differentiating Instruction in a Whole-Group Setting.* Peterborough, NH: Crystal Springs Books.

Santa, C. M., Havens, L. T., & Valdes, B. J. (2004). *Project CRISS: Creating Independence through Student-owned Stategies.* Dubuque, IA: Kendall/Hunt Publishing Company.

BRAIN-BASED INSTRUCTION

• • • Pamela Steward Lowe • • •

BRAIN-BASED INSTRUCTION HAS very specific teaching techniques and strategies designed to optimize the student's learning experience by accessing the brain's need for stimulation and novelty. Students learn best in a stress-free, safe environment, and brain-based instruction exemplifies and maximizes this concept. It helps to reduce the student's fear of error and peer judgment by naturalizing the learning process. The overall classroom environment is strategic and conducive to promoting an open and engaging mind toward learning.

Classroom staging is optimal for brain-based teaching techniques and strategies to work well. Classroom arrangement and atmosphere needs to be open and inviting. Wall colors are carefully chosen in shades of greens or blues in medium to light hues. The choice of colors actually provides a calming effect on students and aids in focus. Classrooms painted in muted, calming colors tend to have fewer instances of student misbehavior and aggression, as has been expressed by documented research. When students are calm and do not feel agitated, it is much easier for them to focus and learn.

Posters are colorful, but not glaringly obtrusive, and are arranged according to subject areas. Most of these posters will remain on the wall all year, so it is important during poster selection to decide which concepts are most important and support the basic skills needed for common core subjects. Some of the less important posters can be changed or replaced during the year as themes, units, and basic skills are added to or introduced. The reasoning behind permanent poster placement is that the brain loves patterns and balance. It relies on recognizable patterns and placement to maximize learning. Students memorize and recall poster placement and the information contained on those posters simply by looking at them day in and day out. A test-taking strategy students are taught to use in brain-based classrooms, during high-stakes testing when posters must be taken down or covered, is to remember the placement of the posters on the wall. Students tend to look up at the space the poster was in and can recall the information it contained during testing. Many times during state standardized testing, I have watched my students stare at the blank wall and then answer the test question, and they have commented on how they could use this technique to picture the answers they were trying to recall.

Brain-based classrooms establish a sense of community among the students. Desks are placed in small groups, and students are encouraged to discuss and share information they are learning. Lessons, assignments, and assessments are a combination of independent works and group collaborations. The goal of this Interactive Instruction Technique is to teach students to not only work independently, but as a contributing member of a group. Students are consistently taught research skills and encouraged to use them. The idea behind this is that if the information or answers can be found by research and using the resources available, then there is less stress on the student to try to commit unnecessary information to memory. If information and details can be found within the resources, the student can focus more on learning and refining basic skills and procedures for problem solving. This makes learning very student friendly and inviting, which is the goal of teaching.

Communication between teachers and students is primary for an atmosphere of acceptance and safety in the classroom. It's important that students feel comfortable talking and sharing with their teacher. Every morning between the time the students arrived, had breakfast, and completed morning work, we spent about 15 to 20 minutes talking and sharing before instruction began. This conversation was based on what we had planned in lessons for the day, asking if there were any concepts they were confused about, any questions they might have, and whether they had any problems with the practices and assignments from the day before. These morning conversations set the tone for the day. The students feel that everyone starts out each day equally and on the same level and the teacher is caring and approachable. These are also optimum times to do a little re-teaching and review for those who have questions or are unsure of the previous day's skills and concepts. Communication techniques such as these allow for a sense of acceptance and community for the students. They come to realize that no question goes unanswered and no question is judged critically.

Brain-based instruction relies heavily on the teacher knowing his/her teaching style and being able to adjust so all student learning styles are met. The teacher needs to observe the students and take notice of their individual learning styles. In doing so, students can be grouped together according to how they learn for some projects and assignments. For instance, the teacher assigns a project to the students using the Independent Study Strategy, divides the students into groups according to their individual learning styles, and tweaks the project outcome for those learning styles. Then the students' products and presentations would not only encompass all their learning needs, but would also be highly diversified and all avenues of the learning experience would be covered. This is differentiation at its most successful.

Teachers need to be aware of the multiple intelligences of their students and design lessons accordingly. The most direct strategy for doing this is through the use of questionnaires and surveys. After discovering what the students are interested in, already know about, or want to know about, the savvy teacher will design and construct engaging lessons that will use this valuable information. Instruction, practice, and product are put into a context that becomes engaging because it is based on the students' interests. The teacher makes the lessons important by using what the students care about as the frame of reference. For example, if a student is interested in becoming a veterinarian, use pets and animals as a vehicle; if they are interested in sports, use sports. Keep instruction and lessons current and varied by keeping in touch with students as their likes and interests change throughout the year. When learning becomes meaningful, students take ownership, and student ownership equates with success in the classroom.

Another meaningful technique used in brain-based classrooms is using the information gained from the questionnaires and surveys to frame questions and examples. Instructional Skills Strategies use a variety of questioning techniques in order to observe and assess student understanding. However, it is important to note that questioning also serves the purpose of clearing up misunderstanding and confusion, and it makes the correct information more solid to the student. Use the student's interests and likes as the framework for questions and in examples which clarify the instruction. Ask a variety of questions from different levels of understanding. Ask fewer simple "yes or no" and single-fact questions and more higher or thinking questions. Encourage students to extend their answers into what they think will happen next, or how it happened. Ask why they answered as they did and how they might do it differently. Brain-based instruction revolves around independent thinking.

Most students avoid answering questions if they can because they are afraid of being wrong. They do not want to risk being judged by their fellow classmates and the teacher. In a brain-based classroom, students are reassured continually that incorrect answers are part of the learning process, because "one must make mistakes in order to learn." Adequate wait time is given without rushing the student; and if the answer is incorrect, the teacher is straight forward and honest in telling the student so, but careful to show no criticism or negative judgment. The questioning technique is equitable in that the teacher does not move on to the next student when an incorrect answer is given, but continues to work with the initial student, giving him/her both verbal and/or written clues and encouragement, bringing the student to the correct answer by providing learning support. This technique is excellent for building trust in the classroom and self-confidence for the student, but primarily it enhances learning.

Direct Instructional Strategies include lecture and explicit teaching, among others. Using the overhead projector, light board, or document camera and Mobi is preferable to the blackboard. The projected space from these medias is more concentrated and promotes student focus because it narrows the field and helps to shut out negative stimulus. The teacher is able to face the students, making eye contact and observing their reactions to the instruction in order to gauge their understanding or confusion. These medias are current and progressive, thus tapping into the students' use, comfortability, and acceptance of new technology. Because the students are focused on the instruction being presented, it is important that the teacher remain with the media being used. Walking around provides a distraction and causes the students' focus to wander, as they are now watching the teacher and this interferes with their concentration.

There are six major concepts in brain-based instruction: (1) provide student focus for learning basic skills, (2) acknowledgement that all subject matter is inter-related and links together during instruction and usage, (3) background knowledge is integral to building a knowledge base and adding to that base, (4) learning support is necessary to learn basic skills and move knowledge from short- to long-term memory, (5) procedures must be taught for problem solving, and (6) review to enhance and promote mastery.

Indirect Instruction Strategies include problem solving, reflective discussion, concept mapping, and reading for meaning, among others. Graphic organizers are an optimal technique used to solidify and enhance the thinking and problem-solving processes. Concept mapping visually shows the relationships of ideas and the inter-relationships they share, whether linear or overlapping. By using these graphic organizers, students are able to visually see, compare and contrast, and reflect on the concepts they are learning. Problem solving is a higher-order thinking skill in all its forms, whether mathematical or literary.

Brain-based classrooms often provide music as a background when students are working. Usually, the music is instrumental and classical or soft listening. Research documents that the connection mathematically between music and thinking optimizes problem solving. Music is repetitious and relies on patterning, which the learning brain recognizes and aligns to.

Repetition, color, and pattern recognition are instructional techniques that can be used throughout all subject areas. For note taking in my classroom, we used either the overhead projector or the document camera. Notes were written down and copied by the students using Direct Instruction. However, the notes were color coded, with each new concept written in a different color, and the students were encouraged to use color, as well. Oftentimes, we added small pictures or diagrams to the margins that had a direct relationship to the subject matter. These techniques helped the students remember the information, as with the posters and standardized testing discussed earlier, students only had to visualize to make a connection to the information and remember.

Other than for practice or drill, worksheets are not a highly used teaching tool. Most assignments are self-created products—assessments the students use to extend their learning and repackage it, demonstrating how much they have mastered through their newly gained knowledge. Rubrics and learning contracts are used, once again, to aid students in taking control and ownership of their learning. By looking through the rubric requirements for projects and assignments, students can choose how much they want to do, but they also know the consequences from the very beginning of the assignment. If they choose to work for a B, then they will receive a B at the culmination of the assignment, no more, no less. Parents are sent a copy of the learning contract, so they, too, are aware of the choices and the amount of work involved. Students may upgrade their contract at any time during the assignment.

Experiential Learning Strategies make great use of experience and background knowledge. Some examples, such as narratives, experiments, role-playing and field trips, provide a deep learning base for students to build on. Thematic instruction and units are techniques that grab the students' desire for firsthand experience and capture their interest. This strategy is very student friendly and non-threatening. There is no great risk involved, just experience. In order for optimal learning to take place, the teacher must give the student a solid base of basic information to build on and then enhance it with extension activities and enrichment.

Students need to realize that learning can be fun, and it is the teacher who sets that tone. To encourage students to complete assignments, I offered free individual computer time, logic games and puzzles, a station with a 500 to 1,000 piece puzzle they could work on between subject instruction, etc. The rule was that the assignment must be finished and turned in before they could do any of these activities, and when I called the class back to order to begin the next subject, they had to stop and immediately return to their desks, ready to learn. This worked very well because it not only kept them motivated and interested, but allowed for choice. Freedom to make choices in the classroom is one of the greatest keys to learning success.

Students need and want to know that what they are learning will be important to them and useable when they are adults. This is another area that brain-based instruction promotes. Students are more receptive to learning when they are told why knowing the skill or information will benefit them and how they will use it as an adult. This brief, sentence or two, explanation was given prior to each new concept that was introduced. Students want their education to have purpose and be related to real life. Once that is established, they will put their minds toward that end and master the concept or procedure as best they can. These instructional techniques and strategies are just a glimpse of all those available from a brain-based perspective for providing students with optimal and successful learning experiences and knowledge.

THE ASSESSMENT-DRIVEN CLASSROOM:
Seven Powerful Ways to Use Assessments to Improve Learning

••• Maxine B. Francis-Gayle, Ph.D •••

IS THERE A DIFFERENCE between assessment and evaluation? These two terms are often used interchangeably but are really quite different in meaning. According to the Center for School Success, *evaluation* is more concerned with comparing the quality of a student's performance, completed assignment, or skillfulness against a standard or other students', while an *assessment* is more focused on providing feedback regarding each student's completed assignment, skillfulness, or performance with the goal of improvement. Evaluation is what occurs yearly as students take high-stakes state tests to determine adequate yearly progress (AYP).

Richard Stiggins (2002) stated that if we, as educators, are to begin to connect the dots between assessment and school improvement in a substantial way, then we have to start looking at assessment with new insight. Educators and students often do not receive the full benefits of assessments because they are either underutilized or inadequately implemented. This chapter will provide educators and homeschool parents with strategies to effectively use assessment to guide their teaching and their students' learning for stronger educational outcomes.

Classroom assessment takes into account everything you, the teacher, does to gather information regarding how your students learn. To fully reap the benefits of using assessments to boost learning, you should spend time getting comfortable with the concept of assessment and be able to express verbally or in writing achievement targets for each of your students. The following seven-step guide will help you begin the process of classroom assessment for learning.

Assessments should be:

1. *Aligned with curriculum and state standards.*

    Become familiar with your state's standards for your content area and grade. Integrate assessments with curriculum (specific learning goals and objectives), instruction, and state standards. Line up the goals and objectives you need to accomplish for a month, grading period, etc., with the assignments and activities you want your students to do to show they understand the concepts you are teaching and are learning. Determine in your head what successful learning should look like, and use the following process as a guide to align your assessments with state and curriculum standards.

    a. The standard I am focusing on is my students' ability to become familiar with a specific task, such as adding fractions, identifying different genres in literature, analyzing data in science, etc., based on information they should already know;

    b. I will ask them to demonstrate their skills by doing a task, such as creating a model, writing a letter, creating a PowerPoint presentation, etc., based on what they should be able to do and/or show how they can apply skills and information learned to new situations;

    c. I will determine mastery of the standard and curriculum objective based on a rubric, checklist, or other means that includes how well my students can explain the concepts and skills being assessed; and

d. I will determine how much time my students are expected to complete the assessment.

2. *Mutually beneficial to both teachers and students.*

Engage your students as partners in their own learning by guiding them to clearly understand their learning objectives, to identify what success looks like, and to link each assignment to their success, regardless of their individual needs. You may have to teach them study skills, organizational skills, using rubrics, and so forth. When you engage your students in their own learning, you open up a great opportunity for them to develop a sense of self-advocacy, self-monitoring, self-managing, and self-modifying. Your students will develop their communication skills in talking about their achievements to both their teacher and their family.

3. *Continuous and not after the fact.*

a. Before you begin any new unit of instruction, one very good assessment practice is to check for prior knowledge. You can do that through a variety of methods such as a pre-test, KWL charts (what students Know, What they need to learn, and what they Learn), and so forth.

b. As you teach, monitor your students' responses and make adjustments to your instruction as you see fit to promote learning. In making adjustments to your instructions, you may realize the need to either increase the pace or slow the pace of instruction, offer remediation, or that students are ready to move on to a new topic.

c. With assessment embedded and ongoing in the classroom, you do not have to wait until the end of a unit to find out that some of your students were completely lost or that a large number understood the information and did not need to spend the time you had allotted for the unit slugging through it, but could move on.

d.   Another aspect of teaching and learning you will become familiar with is that your students learn at different paces and at different depths. In order for you to meet each of their needs, you will find that you need to employ differentiated instruction. That means you could differentiate one or more of the following: content—what you teach; process—how you teach; and product—how your students show what they learn. In other words, you would tailor your instruction to meet the various learning needs of your students, and assessments will help you develop instructional activities that will meet these individual needs.   Again, the goal for this step is to find out what your students are learning and how well they are learning it.

4. *More than student readiness.*

The learning process and your students are complex and multidimensional. Your instruction should as much as possible also align with what your students care about. They tend to learn more readily when that is the case. Your assessments should then focus on ensuring that your students work as often as possible at appropriate levels of challenge.

5. *Beyond formal.*

Assessments do not have to be formal. Whenever you go in search of information regarding student learning, you can use such methods as observation of students to student interactions, student-to-teacher interactions, student journal responses, listening in on small group discussions, observing how students apply instructions to the completion of classroom assignments and projects, anecdotal records, portfolio, and so forth.   Paying attention to your intuition, along with the above, are all methods of assessment that are informal.

6. *More than tests and grade books.*

Keep in mind that the goal of assessment is to increase your students' learning, as well as to sharpen and fine tune your instruction. Therefore, providing your students with consistent and specific feedback (such as, "You did a great job using capitalization," or "You show that you have mastered adding with regrouping") is more productive than just giving them a grade. When you use descriptive versus judgmental feedback, you build your students' confidence and you gain by creating a more productive teaching-learning environment and stronger student-teacher relationship that is built in trust. When you are providing feedback to your students, here are some important points to remember:

a. It is important to give immediate feedback to students while they are still motivated by the objective and topic and can take the appropriate actions, and not when they have forgotten and find the feedback useless. This step includes giving prompt verbal answers to questions, responding immediately to student misunderstandings, and returning tests and assignments within a day or two.

b. Determine how much feedback to give. Give sufficient feedback so students know exactly what to do, but not so much that they feel overwhelmed or you have inadvertently completed the work that is for them. This step includes focusing on as many strengths as the number of weaknesses. Select a couple key areas of weaknesses to highlight, such as commenting on weaknesses important to learning objectives for the unit.

c. Choose the appropriate mode for feedback based on the needs of the student, as well as the format of the assignment. It is best to write feedback that the student needs to keep and be able to refer to on occasion. For students who have difficulties with reading, you may want to give an oral response or written format in a way that it is beneficial for them, such as using a rubric.

d. Think about your audience when you give feedback. How many students need the same response from you? If you have just one student, then have a private conversation; but if you have a small group or most of the class, then address the group as a whole. Your feedback should be differentiated.

e. Focus your feedback on the specific issue at hand, such as a student's attitude toward learning, incomplete assignments, or inappropriate peer interactions during teaching/learning time.

f. Compare students' work, behavior, and so forth to established classroom guidelines and objectives.

g. Remember that the function of feedback is to guide student growth and learning.

h. Be truthful. While the goal is to be positive, do not say something is good when it is not. The goal is to first point out to students how they are progressing toward achieving learning standards and what they need to do improve.

As you get more and more comfortable using assessments to guide the teaching and learning process in your classroom, you will find that you are better able to meet the diverse needs of your students. You will realize that you are more confident and can provide students with multiple avenues to demonstrate their learning of a particular concept. The bonus in moving beyond just testing is that you again encourage your students to become active participants in their own learning by giving them a voice or a say in their learning experience.

7. *Concentrated on strengths.*

As educators, it is so easy for us to develop the need to focus on student weaknesses and brainstorm ways to fix those weaknesses. As you continuously assess your students and classroom practices, focus on their interests, learning styles, and innate strengths and bring those to the surface, instead of focusing on your students' weaknesses. By emphasizing what is positive in your students, you will lay a strong foundation on which their learning can grow and flourish.

At the end of your assessment period, take some time to reflect. Assessment is still about data, whether it is quantitative or qualitative; and in order for it to be beneficial to you and your students, you need to analyze the data. Do not get nervous; we are not talking formal statistics. As a reminder, quantitative data has to do with numbers, which is basically anything you can count or measure, while qualitative data cannot be measured but is more about information you get from observing and what you can describe. Just ask yourself the following questions:

- About students:
  - How many of my students are on target and are learning well? How many are not?
  - Which students are on target? Which ones are not?
  - What strategies are the successful students using that the unsuccessful ones are not?
  - If students are not performing at expected levels, why aren't they?

- About course content:
  - How much material are students actually learning?

- o Which features of the course content are being learned?
- o How much of the original plan was actually taught?
- About teaching:
  - o How does my teaching affect students in a positive way? Negative way?
  - o What specifically would I modify in my teaching to increase learning at all times?

Honest reflection on these questions could be the catalyst for trying new and novel approaches to improve instruction and the learning outcomes of students. In addition, you will have intimate knowledge about what is happening in your classroom, with your students, and be able to confidently articulate this information to administrators and parents.

Historically, significant focus has been placed on the assessment *of* learning resulting in *A Nation at Risk*, NCLB, and a host of school improvement philosophies and strategies that prove to be less than effective. Comparatively, little focus and funding have been given to the development of assessment *for* learning (Stiggins, 2002). As more and more educators begin to grasp the incredible value of assessment for learning and use this strategy, we will begin to see less and less children being left behind.

• • •

References

Brookhart, S.M. (2008). How to give effective feedback to your students. Association for Supervision & Curriculum (ASCD). VA: Alexandria.
www.ascd.org/publications/books/108019.aspx

Center for School Success, http://www.centerforschoolsuccess.org

Fuchs, D. Fuchs, L. S. (2009). Responsiveness to intervention:
multilevel assessment and instruction as early intervention
and disability identify. *Reading Teacher*, (63) 3, 250-252,
November 2009.
http://onlinelibrary.wiley.com/doi/10.1598/RT.63.3.10/abstract

Gaulden, S. (2010). Classroom assessment techniques.
http://www.harford.edu/LAC/pdf%20files/classroom_assess
ment_techniques%20Angelo%20Cross.pdf

Minstrell, J., Anderson, R., & Li, M. (2011). Building on learner
thinking: A framework for assessment in instruction.
http://www7.nationalacademies.org/bose/1STEM_School_Mi
nstrell_Paper_May2011.pdf

Parrish, P.R. & Stodden, R. A. (2009). Aligning assessment and
instruction state standards for children with significant
disabilities. *TEACHING Exceptional Children, (41)* 4, 46-56
Mar-Apr 2009.

Rigby, S. & Dark, M. (2006). Using outcome-based assessment
data to improve assessment and instruction: A case study.
ACM SIGITE Newsletter, (3), 1, 10-15, Jan 2006.
http://dl.acm.org/citation.cfm?id=1113380

Shellard, E. (2005). How assessment data can improve
instruction: When the curriculum is aligned to state
standards, frequent assessments are critical in ensuring that
students are meeting those standards. *Principal*, (84), 3, 30-32,
Jan-Feb 2005.

Stiggins, R.J. (2002): Assessment crisis: The absence of assessment
for Learning. *Phi Delta Kappan*, 2002
http://engageny.org/wpcontent/uploads/2012/08/Assessment
Crisis.pdf

Teacher Vision.
http://www.teachervision.fen.com/assessment/new-
teacher/48353.html#ixzz2CNSr7HU6

Tomlinson, C. A., (2008) Learning to love assessment. *Educational Leadership*, (65), 4, 8-13, Dec-Jan 2008
http://www.ascd.org/publications/educational-leadership/dec07/vol65/num04/Learning-to-Love-Assessment.aspx

COMMON CORE CURRICULUM IN THE ELEMENTARY CLASSROOM

• • • Adele Keaton • • •

HOW CAN I FIT it all in? It's a question many teachers ask. It seems that each year teachers are expected to cover more material in the same amount of time. With the addition of Common Core Curriculum, the time demands have become even greater. There is a solution! By teaching thematically through the content area, you will have additional time and your students will learn more.

The act of teaching language arts in isolation is antiquated. We no longer have time to teach children to read for the sake of reading. We need to use this time not only for reading instruction, but also for teaching content. The challenge for the educator lies in organizing the content and weaving it together between the subject areas.

The first step in this process is to decide upon the essential learning or big idea that you are going to teach. This essential learning can be pulled from science or social studies content. Identify the common core elements that you are going to teach from the common core standards in one of these two areas. The next step is to match those standards with reading and language arts standards in the same grade level. After you have identified the standards that you are going to teach, find books and other materials to teach the content. The final step in the planning process is to decide which skills will be taught with each of the texts. You can then identify best practice activities and exercises that complement the lessons.

One way to bring more content into your classroom is through read alouds. When you are planning your unit, choose books on the topic to read to your students. If you have an ELMO projector, have the students sit close enough to the screen to be able to see what you are reading. Point to the words as you are reading. This will help students acquire sight words. You can also use this time to model reading skills and strategies. When choosing read alouds, look mainly for non-fiction selections. You can also choose a few fiction selections that pertain to the topic and use these fiction stories to teach other common core skills such as plot, characters, inference, etc.

By pairing fiction and non-fiction, the students will continue to strengthen their vocabulary and content knowledge. This is especially important for English language learners and students of lower socioeconomic status. These students tend to struggle with vocabulary. Focusing on a standard and building the classroom theme around this standard will help all of your students gain knowledge and vocabulary in the core content areas.

In addition to blending the core content into reading instruction, you should also match your writing prompts and instruction to the curriculum. Have your students write facts about the topic they have been studying. This allows them to synthesize learning and reinforce the vocabulary that has been introduced to them. Always allow students to look back at the books and other material that they have been using. This teaches them to find facts in informational texts. After reading a fiction selection, students can write about the story and meet core standards, such as retelling, sequencing, planning, editing, revising, organizing, main idea, etc.

Another way you can incorporate this theme learning into your classroom is to select books for a reading center. The easiest way to do this is to look up the Dewey Decimal number of your content area. Visit your school library and select as many books as you can from that section in a variety of reading levels. Display the books in either your read-to-self or read-to-a-buddy area in your classroom. This should be a center that each child is rotated into at some point.

After choosing the books that will be used to teach the unit, consider the key vocabulary students need to know in order to understand the concepts. These words should be taught at the beginning of the unit and reinforced throughout the time that this core standard is being taught. Total Physical Response (TPR) is an ideal way to help students learn vocabulary. The teacher introduces the word and its meaning, and the students then decide on an action to represent that word. They practice the word and the definition with the action. Whenever the word is used in class, the instructor and the students perform the action associated with the word. This is especially good for students who learn through kinesthetic and visual forms of learning.

Adding TPR and other best practices to the unit is the final step in the process of weaving the science or social studies standards with the core curriculum of literacy. Below is an example using a first-grade science unit on organisms. You can adapt this method to your classroom by following the same steps using the standards at the grade level at which you teach.

Example of the Process

The first step is to identify the standards in science or social studies that are going to be taught. For this unit, the identified standard, 1.SF Structure and Function, is from the first-grade curriculum. Students who demonstrate understanding can (b.) Make observations to explain that animals have body parts that they use to obtain and convey information, which the animal responds to with behaviors that help them grow and survive. This particular theme will focus on birds. Next, identify what the students are to learn. The essential learning of this unit could be: My students will understand that birds have feet and beaks which help them protect themselves, build shelters, and feed themselves.

Choosing books to complement and enhance the theme is an important step in this process. The first place to look would be in the 598 section of the library. Pick up field guides, books about individual birds, and books that look like they would be good to read to the class. A few fiction books about birds should also be selected as read alouds. Other fiction books can be added to the reading center. Some possibilities would be Lois Ehlert's *Feathers for Lunch, Bird, Butterfly, Eel* by James Prosek, and *Are You my Mother?* by P.D. Eastman.

Be sure to focus on appropriate vocabulary. This should consist of words that are new to the majority of the students. The vocabulary should make the content of the lessons easier to understand, so you will want to teach the vocabulary at the beginning of the lesson. It is also a good idea to assign movements to the words to further understanding and recollection. The vocabulary for this first-grade unit could include: talons, migration, incubate, beak, nectar, prey, perch, nest, egg, wings, webbed, flight, etc.

The vocabulary can be tied into the introductory lesson. This lesson should build upon the student's background knowledge. Students should be challenged to discuss as much as they know about the subject, which can be recorded in the form of a list or a graphic organizer that can be displayed in the classroom throughout the duration of the unit. Students can also ask questions about the topic. These should also be recorded and checked for understanding at a later date. For this lesson, the teacher would record all of the facts that the children know about birds. The class would print them in an outline of a bird on the interactive whiteboard. Using that outline, we would talk about the parts of the bird. On another screen, the children would name all of the different types of birds they know. We would use this as a starting point, and it would be printed, displayed in the classroom, and added to as the unit progressed. The vocabulary would be discussed with visual cues, and students would create motions to accompany the vocabulary words.

The next step in the process is for the teacher to decide which English language arts standards will be addressed during this unit. For the bird unit, with the combined fiction and non-fiction options, there are many possibilities. Here is a list of the standards that could be covered:

Grade One Reading Standards for Literature K-5

(Only those standards that are applicable will be included.)

1. Ask and answer questions about key details in a text.
2. Retell stories, including key details, and demonstrate understanding of their central message or lesson.
3. Describe characters, settings, and major events in a story, using key details.
5. Explain major differences between books that tell stories and books that give information, drawing on a wide reading range of text types.
6. Identify who is telling the story at various points in a text.
7. Use illustrations and details in a story to describe its characters, setting, or events.
9. Compare and contrast the adventures and experiences of characters in stories.

Reading Standards for Informational Text K-5

1. Ask and answer questions about key details in a text.
2. Identify the main topic and retell key details of a text.
3. Describe the connection between two individuals, events, ideas, or pieces of information in a text.
4. Ask and answer questions to help determine or clarify the meaning of words and phrases in a text.
5. Know and use various text features (e.g. heading, tables of contents, glossaries, electronic menus, icons) to locate key acts or information in a text.

6. Distinguish between information provided by pictures or other illustrations and information provided by the words in a text.
7. Use the illustrations and details in a text to describe its key ideas.
8. Identify the reasons an author gives to support points in a text.
9. Identify basic similarities in and differences between two texts on the same topic (e.g. in illustrations, descriptions, or procedures).
10. With prompting and support, read informational texts appropriately complex for grade one.

Reading Standards: Foundational Skills (K-5)

1. Demonstrate understanding of the organization and basic features of print.
2. Demonstrate understanding of spoken words, syllables, and sounds (phonemes).
3. Know and apply grade-level phonics and word analysis skills in decoding words.
4. Read with sufficient accuracy and fluency to support comprehension.

Writing Standards K-5

1. Write opinion pieces in which they introduce the topic or name the book they are writing about, state an opinion, supply a reason for the opinion, and provide some sense of closure.
2. Write informative/explanatory texts in which they name a topic, supply some facts about the topic, and provide some sense of closure.
3. Write narratives in which they recount two or more appropriately sequenced events, include some details regarding what happened, use temporal words to signal event order, and provide some sense of closure.

After deciding which standards to use, it's time to match the science books to the literacy standards. A good choice to teach the science standard stating that animals respond in order to survive and grow would be the book *Bird, Butterfly, Eel* (realistic fiction). It is a book about migration and how each of the animals comes to the farm in the summer, but migrates to very different areas in the winter. After reading the book, we would ask and answer questions about key details in the text (Reading Standard). The writing assignment to accompany this text would be to describe the connection between two individuals, events, ideas, or pieces of information in a text (Reading Standards for informational text). The students would also use the illustrations and details in the text to describe its key ideas.

Other standards fit well with fiction selections. After reading *Feathers for Lunch*, the students could describe characters, settings, and major events in a story, using key details. They could also retell the story, including key details, and demonstrate understanding of their central message or lesson (Reading Standards). While reading the story, students will know and apply grade-level phonics and word analysis skills in decoding words (Reading Standards: Foundational Skills). During writing time, the children could write narratives in which they recount two or more appropriately sequenced events, include some details regarding what happened, use temporal words to signal event order, and provide some sense of closure (Writing Standard).

For each story, go through the standards to find those that are appropriate and match the text. The final step in the process is to find activities to accompany each of the lessons. Make sure these are rooted in best practice. You could choose a Venn diagram to compare and contrast the three types of animals in the story *Bird, Butterfly, Eel*. As a pre-writing activity for the *Feathers for Lunch* story, I would use a graphic organizer to help the students with the writing process. Another area to look at during this stage in the process is the use of technology and enhancing 21st century skills. For this unit, children could research a bird on the Internet and find a picture of the bird where its beak and feet are visible. They could print a picture of the bird and talk with a partner about what they know about it by looking at the picture.

This last step can make the unit more enjoyable and interesting for your students. By following these steps to create units for your students, you will be able to meet the Common Core Standards in all subject areas. Your students will be challenged by the material, and they will be learning content as they increase their reading skills. It is amazing to see the motivational level for learning increase when thematic teaching is in place. Your students will be talking about television programs they've seen, bringing in books on the subject, and sharing their background knowledge. By creating just one unit, you will see how powerful teaching by this method can be.

INSTRUCTIONAL STRATEGIES FOR THE STRUGGLING LEARNER

How to Reach and Teach Children Who Don't Meet Benchmarks

• • • Deborah B. Circo, M.Ed. • • •

CHILDREN WHO DO NOT reach grade-level benchmarks rightfully demand our attention. These struggling learners need direct instruction targeted to increase and sustain motivation, provide enough practice for mastery, and address multi-modality learning styles. Proficient learners are able to learn with less teacher involvement and with methods such as self-discovery or Socratic questioning techniques. Struggling learners, on the other hand, must be directly, explicitly, and carefully taught in order to progress.

Motivation

Struggling learners often have a past riddled with academic failure. They may react to this past by disinterest, loss of attention to instruction, and behavioral issues. They may say, "This is boring!" This state of mind leads to students who are unavailable for learning. The following techniques motivate and engage these and all students in the learning process.

Begin a challenging lesson with movement. Simple stretching at the desk can invigorate the brain and increase blood flow. Prepare the eyes for tracking words by a simple figure-eight exercise: Students clasp their hands together, move their hands across their bodies in a figure-eight pattern, and track the hands with their eyes without moving their head. Deep breathing is beneficial: instruct the students to put their tongue on the roof of their mouth and closing the mouth, breathe through the nose: "Breathe in—one, two, three, four; breathe out slowly—one, two, and three.

Introduce a lesson by connecting the purpose with the learner's prior knowledge. For example, the teacher says, "We have learned the vowel sound /e/. Today, we will read and spell words with /e/. This will help you every day in your work." A short, simple statement is best.

Use a marble jar. To give students credit for being active learners, drop a marble into a glass jar. Many teachers use the marble jar for classroom management. When the jar is full, the class earns a reward, such as a popcorn party. Use of the marble jar in instruction is different in that many more marbles are given. As the marble drops into the glass jar, it produces a sound. This sound will sustain interest and attention as it works to keep the brain alert. The jar may be a group jar or individual small jars. The teacher may add a comment occasionally, such as, "Great effort," or "Good answer." Limit and then phase out the comments, though, so instruction is not impacted. You may wish to choose a reward system to link to the number of marbles acquired. (See reward card system below.)

Use a reward card system. This is a plain 3 x 5 card that the student writes her name on and keeps on her desk. Draw a star or use a stamp on the card as you catch student involvement. When the card is full, the student can trade it in for a classroom privilege or small reward. As an alternative when working with older students, have students mark their own cards using tally points. This is helpful when you are teaching a large group because you can tell the student, "Great, give yourself a point." Instruction is less interrupted. If you wish to use a pre-printed card for younger children, an example is in Appendix A.

Have students keep records of their own progress. Use simple charts that the learner fills in at the end of the lesson. Younger children can self-evaluate by circling different faces to show how they think they did. See Appendix B for a simple example. Older children can keep bar graphs to show their growth on a skill.

Use a learner-controlled prop during instruction. I have often used small stuffed animals. Toss one to a student to engage him when you see involvement flagging. Stress balls and porcupine balls work great, as well, and can be easily sterilized. Have a standing rule that you will remove the prop if it becomes distracting.

These simple techniques can help struggling learners experience academic success. They experience success as they learn that it is possible to focus on instruction. They experience the satisfaction of being actively involved in the learning process.

Practice for Mastery

Struggling learners require a greater amount of repetition and practice to master new learning. Some publishers have incorporated the needed practice into their explicitly scripted teacher guides. If you are not using this type of curriculum, the following instructional strategies will help you increase the number of times your learners practice the concept.

Incorporate a very high student response rate into your instruction. Follow a pattern in which the teacher states the information in a brief statement and students repeat the statement when cued. For example, teacher states, "This word is 'teach'—what word?" Students respond, "Teach." Teacher says, "Spell 'teach'." Students say, "t-e-a-c-h." Teacher says, "What word?" Students say, "Teach!" Six repetitions have taken place in a short amount of time.

Thumbs up, thumbs down: students respond to a teacher's cue by putting their thumbs up or down. For example, "If you agree with Jose's answer, thumbs up. Disagree? Thumbs down!" This requires students to pay attention to the responses of others, which increases their own practice and repetitions toward mastery. Students should be taught to keep their fist against their chest to show their thumb so that others cannot see how the one giving the answer is judged. When the answer is incorrect, teacher may say, "Good try, Jose. The answer is _____. Everyone, say it." This helps shelter the learner's self-esteem while providing the correction.

Provide written practice that has many repetitions. For example, when practicing a sight word or spelling word, the word is printed in large lower case letters on the worksheet. Students then trace the word with three colors while saying the spelling out loud. Next, the students print the word largely and trace it (on the letter, not around the letters) with three different colors. Lastly, the students fold the paper so the word is hidden and write it from memory. This has provided eight repetitions of the word.

Practice individually with students. The following is a successful method I have developed for practicing sight words and math facts. The student has a stack of five to ten words/facts they are working to master. Follow these steps:

1. Show the student each card and say, "This word says teach. Say 'teach'." Student repeats the word.

2. Place the cards face up on the table. Touch and say each word. Student touches and says each word, modeling you.

3. Now, say, "Touch each word I say and say it." You will say words in random order so that the student must scan all the words while looking for the targeted word. Correct mistakes by saying, "That word says 'learn.' Find 'teach'. What does it start with?"

4. Re-arrange the words and repeat #3 as often as needed for correct answers or as time permits.

5. End by checking the learning. Gather the cards and ask the student to read each card independently. Mark a tally mark on the back of each correctly given card. You will continue to practice the words with the student at other sessions until ten

tally marks are earned. I often give tally marks for the practice in the "find and touch" session, as well.

This activity can also be used for math facts. The answer is written with the equation on one side of the card, but omitted on the other side. The omitted side is used as the test at the end of the session.

This instructional strategy has provided from eight to many more repetitions, depending on time. Consider teaching this method to parent volunteers since it is so individualized. A simple script card is provided for you to copy as a reference in Appendix B.

It has been said that it takes the average learner twenty repetitions to master new learning. Our struggling students require many, many more. As you give your students plenty of opportunities to practice, you will see more of them meeting benchmarks and experiencing academic success.

Multi-Modality Instruction

The mode of instruction refers to the channel that the instruction is processed through. The instruction may be offered and practiced through the visual, auditory, tactile, and kinesthetic modes. Groups of learners have a variety of processing strengths and weaknesses in these areas. Therefore, the most effective instructional practices target more than one mode at a time. Many struggling students have strengths in the tactile and kinesthetic modes. Targeted practice that uses both touch and movement will have greater impact. The visual mode is often stronger than the auditory mode, so visual input paired with spoken input is essential.

The following are instructional strategies that employ multi-modality instruction:

Many excellent computer programs and apps provide visual/auditory/kinesthetic input and practice tailored to each individual student. Monitor closely, however, since interest and attention can be variable. Get advice from trusted colleagues on which programs and apps are most effective.

Students write answers on small whiteboards and stand to show their answer.

Students create movements that are used when spelling out loud, practicing math facts, repeating directions and concepts, etc. The learner looks at the visual image of the word or fact. Girls enjoy pretending they are cheerleaders while practicing.

Student writes a word or fact with a crayon on a piece of paper that has been laid on a piece of rough sandpaper. Student says the letters or numbers out loud while writing. After the response is written, more tactile input is gained when the bumpy response is then traced with a finger.

Student writes a word or fact in a salt tray. Make a simple salt tray by pouring salt into a cookie sheet that has raised sides. Provide a large image of the word. This is a great center activity.

Provide a direct instruction lesson using directed drawing the student then labels with key vocabulary or writes about, depending upon the level of the student.

Students look at a flash card and toss a bean bag to a partner while reciting the flash card information.

Good teachers strive to teach to their students' strengths. Classrooms have students with such a wide range of strengths that it makes good sense to use multi-modality instruction. This gives each student an opportunity to practice learning as an active, engaged learner.

Summary

You will make learning more accessible for struggling students when you employ the proven strategies listed above. Struggling learners require many more repetitions to master a concept. Employing strategies that motivate, provide direct instruction, and give more opportunities to practice and reach students in a variety of modalities within your lessons will make a difference in student success. Struggling students can become confident students who look forward to learning.

Appendix A: Reward Card Examples

This is an example of a simple reward card for motivating younger students. Draw stars in the boxes, use a small stamp, or use stickers. Link a completed card to a reward such as free time,

A blank 3" x 5" requires no preparation. Students simply write their names on the card. Older students can be given the responsibility to give themselves a tally point when directed. Again, completed cards are turned in for a reward.

Appendix B: Learning Chart for Self-Evaluation

Name: Date: How did you do today?

This is an example of a simple self-evaluation tool. Older students can use graph paper to make bar graphs showing progress.

Appendix C: Individualized Sight Word/Math Facts Practice (change wording for math facts)

Individualized Directed Practice

1. Show the student each card and say, "This word says _____. Say _____." Student repeats the word.

2. Place the cards face up on the table. Touch and say each word. Student touches and says each word.

3. Now, say, "Touch each word I say and say it." Say words in random order. Correct mistakes by saying, "That word says _____. Find _____. What does it start with?"

4. Re-arrange the words and repeat #3.

5. Gather the cards. Show student each card. Place a tally mark on the back of each correctly given card.

INSTRUCTIONAL STRATEGIES FOR ADD/ADHD STUDENTS

• • • Cheryl Caddell-Savage • • •

What is Wrong With Me?

AS A CHILD, I did not understand that I had a learning disability—I just thought I was not very smart. I remember being in fifth grade and having to create a physical map of the United States – you know, the one made from flour and water. Oh, no! The teacher had to call the custodian to scrape my map off the floor. I was so embarrassed! Nobody else had this problem – just me. This is only one incident from my struggles in school.

Later, when in college, I realized I really did have a learning problem—a problem with processing and comprehending lots of material. Later, I was diagnosed with ADD. Wow! Okay, so now I knew and could learn ways to compensate for this. I realized that I managed without any problems until I entered the fifth grade. I remembered as a child that I always sat with my mother at the kitchen table while doing my homework. My sister was there, too, but I realized I was the one who took so much individual time to complete assignments. My mother passed away with cancer when I was ten—when I was just beginning fifth grade. Suddenly, I began to see the problem. Mom must have realized I had difficulty focusing and comprehending too much information at one time. There were six of us children, and Dad had to work to provide for us, so he didn't have the time to become aware that I needed extra help.

The trial and error of my experiences and discovery of my disability have helped me understand how students learn. I am very drawn to the students I see struggling as I did and are not yet aware of their problem or how to compensate for it. As a teacher, I focused on curriculum integration with lots of team work and implementation of the arts. I find team work is so important in order to build trusting relationships among students and allow them to see the talents offered by each member. With this in mind, I would like to share ideas for instructional strategy techniques for those with ADD and ADHD, along with an idea of a lesson plan incorporating the arts and meeting the needs of different learning styles.

Strategies:

- Colored Overlays: This is a strategy used by a lot of resource teachers. I was introduced to this by Christine Crawford, a resource teacher in Charleston, SC, while teaching fifth grade. The idea is to use colored overlays to cover specific material, such as multiple-choice or fill-in-the-blank assessments, literature, math problems, etc., so the student is not overwhelmed by too much print. Among the benefits for this technique are improved comprehension and an increase in reading, *Dr. Greg Robinson, Applied Psychology Unit, Cambridge University.*

- Sheet Sliding: This is the same principle as colored overlays, but it can be used with regular paper. I would use this so the student could only see a certain portion of the material and, therefore, feel less stress about the amount of work to complete. This allows you to have the student complete a certain amount until you can come back to them and check what they have accomplished. Covering the material with paper helps calm the student and allows them to focus only on what they see.

- Highlighters: I could not have survived college without this technique. I would highlight different material or concepts with different colors. During the test, I could close my eyes and actually see the material in color and be able to assess well. This truly saved me in college! In my classroom, whenever students took notes or studied in their teams, highlighters were on the desk and ready for use. Teaching this strategy early on will help students be successful throughout their school years.

Techniques:

- Activity Options: One of the best ways to get students involved with their learning is to ask for their input in regard to new concepts you will be teaching. I accomplished this by webbing (using a graphic organizer) the next unit on the board. After listing major concepts of the unit, we would discuss what they would like to do (activities) to address these concepts. This gave the students a sense of empowerment—they wanted to be successful and accomplish these goals. Keep in mind that some of their suggestions may not be feasible – but acknowledge all and let the students know that as a class you will accomplish as much as possible within this unit and time frame.

- Activities/Assessments (both) can be assessed by choice of product. This can be accomplished through making a brochure, creating a PowerPoint, hands-on experiments, class presentations, traditional assessments, and many more. Try to mix it up so you address all learning styles.

- Identifying Learning Styles: If possible, pass out a learning style sheet at the beginning of the year so you can learn the students' most effective way of learning. Refer to Howard Gardner's' Multiple Intelligences: http://www.discover-multiple-intelligences.com.

- Know YOUR Teaching Style: Is your teaching style impacting your students learning? This is so important. I have presented many workshops on this topic. It is so much fun when teachers realize they teach to their learning style (direct instruction, note taking, etc.) and do not implement other techniques. Check to see if you do more than one type of teaching style and then gradually work on incorporating the other styles.

Sample lesson of arts integration with the curriculum and meeting different learning styles:

Slavery Vs. Freedom	
Grade Level: 4th	**Time Allotted:** 2 weeks
Lesson Overview Write a summary of the lesson plan.	
The study of the Civil War – slavery vs. freedom. Students will compare and contrast the two. Understand the emotions that slaves must have felt by actually dramatizing scenes from the book *Henry's Freedom Box* by Ellen Levine. They will retell the story of Henry and discuss the emotions of slaves.	
Goals What are the goals or objectives for this lesson? What should the students be able to do at the conclusion of the lesson?	
Goals: Integrating drama with movement and music to help students express and feel the emotions of others. Write a new ending to the story of Henry. Create tableaus (freeze frames) of beginning, middle and end of a story. Create a 3-page PowerPoint presentation about a point of view – slavery vs. freedom. Create a replica of the box in which Henry traveled to freedom. Paint a picture of one of the scenes from *Henry's Freedom Box* for class presentation.	

Standards
Common Core Standards and the NETS Standards (ISTE)
that this lesson directly addresses.

Standards:
Reading Standards:
Key Ideas and Details:
3. Describe in depth a character, setting, or event in a story or drama, drawing on specific details in the text (e.g. a character's thoughts, words, or actions).
Integration of Knowledge and Ideas:
7. Make connections between the text of a story or drama and a visual or oral presentation of the text, identifying where each version reflects specific description texts to support analysis, reflection, and research.

Writing Standards:
Research to Build and Present Knowledge:
9. Draw evidence from literary or informational texts to support analysis, reflection, and research.
    a. Apply *grade 4 reading standards* to literature (e.g., Describe in depth a character, setting, or event in a story or drama, drawing on specific details in the text [e.g., a character's thoughts, words, or actions] and directions in the text.

Speaking and Listening Standards:
Comprehension and Collaboration
2. Paraphrase portions of a text read aloud or information presented in diverse media and formats, including visually, quantitatively, and orally.

Presentation of Knowledge and Ideas
4. Report on a topic or text, tell a story, or recount an experience in an organized manner, using appropriate facts and relevant, descriptive details to support main ideas or themes; speak clearly at an understandable pace.

Arts:
Visual Arts: Space and Form

Drama: **Acting by assuming roles and interacting in improvisations**
Benchmark 1
- Imagine and clearly describe characters, their relationships, and their environments
- Assume roles that exhibit concentration and contribute to the action of classroom dramatizations based on personal experience and heritage, imagination, literature, and history
- Become comfortable performing in front of an audience
- Retell/ perform stories, poems, songs, tales
- Develop expression using the body, voice, and gestures

Designing by visualizing and arranging environments for classroom dramatizations

Benchmark 1
Collaborate to establish playing spaces for classroom dramatizations and to select and safely organize available materials that suggest scenery, properties, lighting, sound, costumes, and makeup

Math: **Draw and identify lines and angles and classify shapes by properties of their lines and angles**
1. Draw points, lines, line segments, rays, angles (right, acute, obtuse), and perpendicular and parallel lines. Identify these in two-dimensional figures.

NETS.S
1. Facilitate and Inspire Student Learning and Creativity
   c. Promote student reflection using collaborative tools to reveal and clarify students' conceptual understanding and thinking, planning, and creative processes

2. Design and Develop Digital Age Learning Experiences
and Assessments

   c. Customize and personalize learning activities to
   address students' diverse learning styles, working
   strategies, and abilities using digital tools and resources.

Materials

Book *Henry's Freedom Box* by Ellen Levine; music that
represents moving through the woods in a secretive,
scary way; poster paper, water colors, paint brushes, cups
for water, and paper towels; use of a computer for the
PowerPoint, books for student research related to the Civil
War; index cards with specific scenes posted for student
freeze frames; paper for new ending of the book *Henry's
Freedom Box* by Ellen Levine.

Boxes provided from home or teacher resources

Technology: PowerPoint for presentations

Search engines for research

Activities

Teacher Activities	Student Activities
The teacher will introduce concepts of the Civil War using literature and other resources.	Drama: Using movement and music, the students will act out the book about Henry.
Read the book about Henry and discuss the emotions slaves felt and how Henry felt.	Drama: Students will create freeze frames of scenes from the book about Henry.
Teacher guidance of research for presentation for slavery vs. freedom.	Math & Arts: Students will create replica of the box in which Henry was shipped.
Direct teams for box replica of Henry's Freedom Box	Arts: Students will create a painting of one of the scenes from the book.

	ELA: Write a new ending to the story of Henry ELA & SS: PowerPoint on slavery vs. freedom
Assessments: Brochures, PowerPoint, Presentation, Traditional Assessments, etc.	

VISUAL STRATEGIES

• • • Helen Sauer • • •

STUDENTS LEARN IN A wide variety of ways. The focus of this chapter is using visuals to support children who struggle with comprehension throughout their school day. I will present some visuals strategies to help those who struggle and make their learning more successful.

These are strategies I have used throughout my years of teaching students with mild to significant disabilities. The strategies are for any student who needs the support to make the connection between what they hear and understanding. Keep in mind that the visuals you will read about here are examples of what can be done, and they can be adapted or modified to meet an individual's needs.

The majority of the visuals you'll read about in this chapter on created in a software program called Boardmaker Plus v.6 from Mayer-Johnson. It's not necessary to have a software program to create the pictures. You can create pictures to meet your needs using a camera, if you like photographs. I have used pictures from the Internet. I'd Google what I was looking for and then click on images.

Many students like to see the daily schedule. They don't need details within each subject, but like to know the order of their day. Times could be added, if desired. Picture words can be put in a schedule format, vertical or horizontal. Pictures are laminated and velcroed to the schedule strip. This way, only one strip is needed and pictures can be moved around, as needed. Materials needed are a laminated strip of construction paper the appropriate length for the number of pictures, laminated subject picture/words, recess, lunch pictures and the like, and Velcro.

Some students need motivation to complete their assignments and also want to know when they will be done. The first one has a picture and the words I am working for: a picture of the student's choice goes on top, showing what they may do when done. Three Velcro spots can be used to put pictures of work to be done under the top picture. As each assignment is done, it can be removed. When the card is done, the student may do the activity of choice. You might also choose to have three tokens with Velcro. As the student completes work, he is given a token. When three have been earned, the student gets to do the chosen activity. If you want more or less things to be done, the card can have more or less spaces. Materials needed are a piece of laminated construction paper, approximately 4 x 6 or the size you want, the pictures mentioned and/or tokens, and Velcro. Laminate any pictures you use.

The next one has slots for three assignments, numbered 1, 2, 3, and a last space which shows the sign for "all done" with the words. There is a piece of plastic attached so pictures can be slipped in. The second row shows 1st and then with picture/words. This helps when working on the concept of first you do_____, then you do_____. The last item in the row is a pocket with picture/ words of all done. As work is done, pictures are stored in the pocket. Materials needed are a piece of tag board large enough to hold the schedule, numbers 1,2,3, pictures of work to be done, all done, first, then, library pocket to put completed pictures in, and Velcro.

Some students have difficulty working in a timely manner. A visual timer can be set for up to an hour. It runs quietly. Red covers the set time period, and then as the time decreases, the red gets smaller. When the red is gone, time is up. The timer comes in a variety of sizes, from 3 inches to 12 inches, a size useable for the entire class. Google visual timer, and then go to images, and you'll find a wide variety. You can also set a timer. The basic difference is the visual timer is quiet.

Students don't always know what it looks like to be ready to learn. Below are two examples of what it looks like to be ready. I got these ideas from working with a speech language therapist. The first one can be used with the entire class. The second one I've put by specific students who need reminders frequently. The first one says "Good Listening!" Under that, it says, "I listen with my whole body." The top two pictures say, "I'm ready to work" and "My eyes are on the teacher." The next lines reads, "I listen with my ears" and "My feet are quiet." The last line is, "My hands are quiet and "My mouth is quiet." Materials needed are the six pictures with the captions mentioned and an 8 x 11sheet of paper. I make this using Board Maker. Pictures and wording are sized to fill the sheet.

The second one is shorter. The top picture reads, "I'm ready to work." The next line says, "Sit quietly, eyes on teacher, listen." The bottom line reads, "!quiet hands, no noises from mouth, quiet feet." Pictures are included with each caption. Pictures are smaller as this visual is for use with one or two students at a time.

Next is a sample of class rules with picture cues. Rules are simple and short, such as:

1.Sit in my seat
2. Raise my hand
3. Soft voice
4. Do my work
5. Be kind

I've used a stop light for behavior. When all three lights are on, behaviors are appropriate. If green comes off, that's the first warning. Yellow is the second warning, and red is the final warning. If the red comes off, there is a consequence for the behavior. For other students, the consequence comes with the red light. All students may have one, or specific students may have one. I found the stop light on the Internet and then used laminated colored dots for the lights.

These next idea uses two pictures, depicting expected behaviors, especially if an inappropriate behavior is being displayed. The first example shows a student wiggling with a line through it. An arrow points from the first picture to a picture of the student standing quietly next to him. Centered over both pictures are the words "stand quietly." Another example is a picture of a student tantruming and a student next to him who is calm and happy. A large arrow above the pictures points from the first to the second student. The words"calm down" are centered above the students at the top of the page. When a student sees what is expected, many times he/she is able to do what is shown.

The last examples depict some common behaviors we expect from our students. The visual cue acts as a reminder of what is expected. Small pictures of specific behaviors can be on a student's desk. When a reminder is needed , the teacher walks by, taps a picture and moves on. It's a quiet way to remind students what they need to be doing.

The first depicts a student sitting ar his desk working, with the caption "do my work." This can be used with a student who has difficulty staying focused on his work. Some students have difficulty being quiet. A picture of a face with the index finger to the mouth, indicating "quiet mouth," can be used. The last example is for lining up. The picture shows students standing in line, facing forward, hands to their sides and quiet mouths. Put on the door or where the students line up, it's a great reminder of how they should look.

These examples are but the tip of the iceberg when it comes to the possibilities of when to use visual supports. Another way to use visual supports is with vocabulary. Pictures that support concepts in reading , science, social studies, and math greatly enhance the learning of those students struggling with the concepts because they can't make sense of what they are hearing or reading.

It's amazing what you'll be able to create for your struggling students once you jump in and give it a try. The more you do it, the easier it becomes, and you soon you'll have built a repetoire of visuals to use year after year with the curriculum.

If you are interested in picture samples of what I have described or have any questions, you may contact me at my email: sauerhs @ bridgemail.com.

GOAL SETTING USING STUDENT DATA

• • • Dr. Brooks Thomas • • •

SCHOOL IS DIFFICULT. BEING a student is difficult. Being a kid is difficult. There are always bumps in the road. Sometimes it seems too difficult or too overwhelming to get started, much less to continue on the learning path. A map is the ancient tool used to guide a traveler on a difficult journey. The best tool an educator and a student can have to ensure a prosperous journey is a map consisting of well-designed goals to direct learning. Goal setting is a life skill that, when done effectively, can make the pursuit of knowledge efficient and personal. Goal setting can give the learner a sense of responsibility and ownership of the learning path.

An astute classroom practitioner must first know their students emotionally. Building relationships is paramount to a successful learning environment. The cultural expectations and physical surroundings also contribute to the qualitative dimension of the learning environment. The teacher begins the year with carefully designed learning goals, molded through deep knowledge of system-adopted standards. However, there is one component in thriving student-centered classrooms that is often overlooked. The savvy 21st century classroom instructor must teach students how to set their own academic goals. This is accomplished by using qualitative, as well as quantitative, data to get to know each student and assist each student in knowing themselves deeply. The following is a road map for developing the habit of goal setting. This habit, when ingrained completely, will help students to become lifelong learners.

Students Gain Self-Knowledge

Ownership of a goal is very important. Students who set clear workable goals see themselves as part of the learning process. Start with data particular to each student. In this data-rich time, most school systems provide teachers access to longitudinal data covering the student's entire school history. Show students this data. Share their history with them and allow them to graph their progress over the years. Below is an example of a crude, yet personal, account of a student's state test results, coupled with other district adopted achievement results.

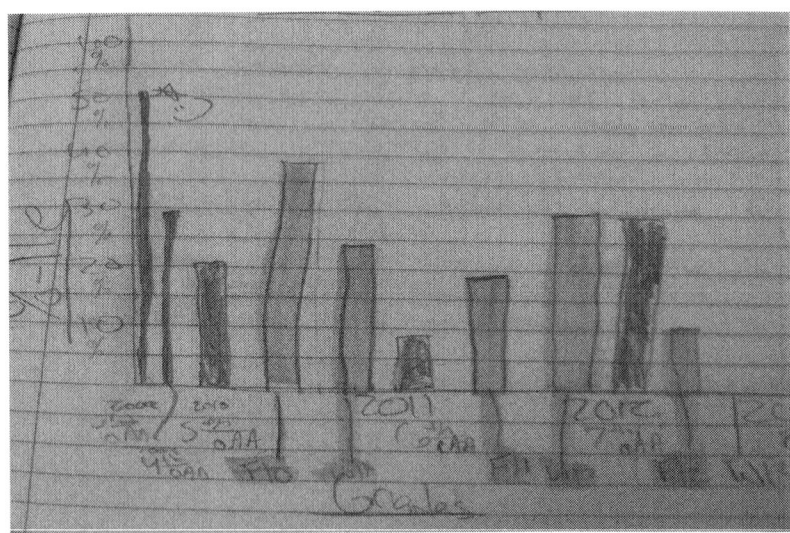

During the process of mapping their history, students are able to make insightful observations concerning their progress over the years. Comments generated as students explore their history allow the teacher to understand how students interpret their progress, or lack thereof. The teacher can also clear up any misconceptions about the use of test results or data interpretation. In addition, the teacher can help the student understand that student data is collected and available for their educational planning. Most students show a degree of pride when they realize there is a database reflecting their educational development.

Create a Vision

The next task the teacher may perform to assist students in goal setting is to use data from the past to help students plan their future. Creating a visual representation of student progress makes the sterile records of student achievement morph into something exceptionally personal. While technology can be used to create a polished picture of student progress, the coarse methodology of hand-drawn graphs can make ownership of the profile more meaningful. Either way, students keep notebooks or portfolios to record class work. Allow this graphic data analysis to become part of student notebooks so they have their own record of their data. Students may refer to the past while planning the future when the information is readily available to them. Students can present this visual product to parents at conferences or use it to plan projects with other students. With a clear vision of their own record of learning and the standards by which they are measured, students can conceive of learning as their own personalized journey.

Goal Setting as a Motivational Tool

Once the student is comfortable with mapping their past progress, teachers can help students organize their path to reaching future goals. Help the learners analyze their data. Listen closely to the conversations and provide input when needed. A common misconception for students and teachers is the difference between percentile results on achievement tests and percentile scoring in the classroom. A discussion about 50th percentile being the "average" student score will help clear the confusion. In school, we tend to view 85 percent as a letter grade of B and 50 percent as a failing grade. Most students need a lesson on percentile scores as presented in achievement test results. Also, show students how to use value added for measuring personal growth. Students and teachers need to understand that movement from the 45th percentile to the 48th percentile is growth. Growth and improvement are the goal. Once you have trained your students on how to search for their personal progress, they will learn to measure their growth and become motivated toward improvement. Older students may select high school classes based on their understanding of their strengths, weaknesses, and interests reflected in the data history. Setting personal goals based on individual performance is a life skill worth teaching well.

Flexibility is Important

Adaptability is another problem-solving skill worth direct instruction. If you notice that your students are not referring to their data or using their set goals, allow them to change the process or the product. If hand-drawn data tables are not working, place the data on a spreadsheet. If the goal setting seems impersonal, encourage students to reword their goals. One student voiced concern that her writing was boring. Upon reviewing her writing goals set the month before, one goal read: *I will use variety in sentence beginnings and sentence structure.* After a brief discussion, she reworded the goal as follows: *I will make my writing more interesting by using different beginnings and lengths for my sentences.* The truth is the first goal was written with heavy assistance from the teacher. When the student began looking at her writing through a more critical lens, the goals became more important to her. She wrote the second goal by herself. It took time for this student to own her goals, but she developed a belief that it is important to make writing entertaining. This was a multi-step process, but the product is a motivated, responsible, and involved writer.

Goal setting using student data will clarify learning for students and teachers. Students with a clear vision of past progress are more likely to take control of their future. Know that the path to using student data to create goals may need to be altered along the way. This relieves the pressure of getting it right the first time. If students know that they are in control of their learning, they will be less stressed, more motivated, and more involved. After all, student involvement is the number one component to effective instruction and measurable, lasting student learning.

CRITICAL FRIENDS GROUPS AS A METHOD OF IMPROVING TEACHER PRACTICE

• • • Dr. Crystal Rende • • •

PROFESSIONAL DEVELOPMENT (PD) IS essential to school reform due to the push for increases in student achievement, changes in standards, and adjustments to the teacher evaluation systems used in most school districts. As a result, teachers are facing more and more professional development requirements. "Despite the general acceptance of professional development as essential to improvement in education, reviews of professional development research consistently point out the ineffectiveness of most programs" (Guskey, 2002, p. 381). In fact, many PD programs are not meaningful in their content, nor do they sustain any long-term impact when teachers return to their classrooms (Guskey, 2000). Grover Whitehurst (2002), former Assistant Secretary for Education Research and Improvement for the U. S. Department of Education, supported Guskey's findings and discussed the impact of PD on student achievement in his article entitled "Improving Teacher Quality." In this article, he stated that the body of research on teacher preparation and professional development is a long way from the stage of converging evidence and professional consensus. Whitehurst further argued for PD that emphasized intense, content-focused experiences, peer collaboration, and structured induction experiences for new teachers. Most PD programs are presented outside of the daily practice through workshops or other models that are not ongoing and embedded in the daily practice of participants (Eaker, 2002).

High-quality PD involves more than a one-time exposure to strategies presented in a workshop or in a one-day session. Unfortunately, this is often what teachers experience (Guskey, 2000). Teachers invest time in these experiences with the hope of walking away with something tangible that they can implement immediately, but are often left disappointed with their experiences or unable to fully implement what they have learned. The American Federation of Teachers (AFT) (2002) released guidelines for creating professional PD programs that make a difference in schools. The AFT found that there were eleven principles for high quality professional development. The principles stated that PD should:

1. Deepen and broaden knowledge of content.

2. Provide a strong foundation in the pedagogy of particular disciplines.

3. Provide knowledge about the teaching and learning processes.

4. Be rooted in and reflect the best available research.

5. Be aligned with the standards and curriculum that teachers use.

6. Contribute to measurable improvement in student achievement.

7. Be intellectually engaging and address the complexity of teaching.

8. Provide sufficient time, support, and resources to enable teachers to master new content and pedagogy and to integrate this knowledge and skill into their practice.

9. Be designed by teachers in cooperation with experts in the field.

10. Take a variety of forms, including some we have not typically considered.

11. Be job-embedded and site specific (AFT, 2002, p. 11-12).

The real purpose of PD programs is to cause change in the classroom practices of teachers. Specifically, PD should change teachers' attitudes and beliefs and the learning outcomes of their students (Guskey, 2002). Perhaps it is time that the PD be put in the hands of the teachers and their colleagues.

In an effort to advance school models of PD and enhance decision-making practices, school districts have been implementing programs that establish professional learning communities (PLCs) within their schools (DuFour, 2006). The premise of PLCs is that all community members (teachers, administrators, students, parents, etc.) work collaboratively to move the school in a direction that ultimately improves student performance. PLCs involve a range of PD programs and tools. The establishment of Critical Friends Groups (CFGs) is one strategy of a PLC. CFGs consist of a group from the school community that comes together to critically reflect on their daily practices. *The Looking At Student Work* (LASW) model is an example of a CFG (Blythe and Allen, 1999).

The impact that LASW programs or critical friends groups can have on teaching is vast. The actual extent to which they impact the practice is really unknown. However, it is clear that collaboration among teachers allows them to feel a sense of security and support, which is greatly needed in a time when new common core standards and teacher evaluation systems are increasing the demands on teachers. The practice of teaching in isolation without interaction with colleagues is outdated and will not benefit those teachers who are facing new standards and evaluations. The trick is to make the PD time useful and enable teachers to work in small groups to reflect, analyze, and plan.

Blythe, Allen, and Powell (1998) first introduced the LASW protocol method (Appendix A and B) in the book titled *Assessing Student Learning: From Grading to Understanding*. The book was part of an effort to begin changing the ways in which teachers examine and evaluate student work. As an extension of the first book, the authors created a second book in 1999, entitled *Looking Together at Student Work*. This second book, which more closely examined the process of collaborative reflection and introduced a variety of protocols that can be used in collaborative meetings, led to the establishment of LASW websites and learning communities across the country.

In an ongoing effort to increase student achievement, schools have further explored the idea of teachers' impact on student learning. This has resulted in a need for teachers to actively think about what students understand and how students apply what is taught in the classroom every day. Such a process must be done quickly and effectively so the valuable instructional time teachers have with their students is not wasted. Teachers need support in developing the skills necessary to complete these tasks. The LASW association (www.lasw.org, accessed June 21, 2009) suggested that programs such as theirs provide that support to teachers by qualified facilitators when the program is implemented. The LASW association's program model consists of a series of collaborative sessions involving teachers and other stakeholders in examining student artifacts using either the Collaborative Assessment Protocol (Appendix A) or the Tuning Protocol (Appendix B) (Blythe, 1999). The immediate outcome of the session is an action plan that can be implemented the following class day and reflected and reported on at the next meeting (Blythe, 1999). The LASW program is informed by the following seven principles:

1. *Value: Student work is often serious work and is intentional. Members of the school community should value this work as such and use it to improve instruction.*

2. *Inquiry: When using student work, it is important to look for what can be learned from the product, rather than to simply look for what is wrong. This should result in a process that goes beyond assigning a grade.*

3. *Collaboration: The work of schools has historically been very private; however, it is important to reverse this norm and eliminate isolation within the school setting.*

4. *Reflection: To improve instruction, it is important to look at student work in depth and collaboratively, over time, and to engage in reflective dialogue about the work, the child(ren), and teaching and learning.*

5. *Aligned Purpose: When looking collaboratively at student work, it is important to have a common purpose or goal so that the process is reflective of this goal.*

6. *Standards: When discussing and examining student work, it is important to consider standards of all levels, including state and national standards.*

7. *PLC Connections: The process of examining student work can be one way to strengthen connections between children's learning and changes in instruction, curriculum, or other aspects of school life and is, therefore, one tool in building PLCs* (LASW website, 2009).

The research completed by Dunne (2000) shows that collaboration is the key to improving schools' performance in all areas. The LASW program creates an environment that provides time for collaboration, facilitation in the process of collaboration, and protocols to ensure sessions occur in a manner that results in a usable product. However, limited research has been done on evaluating the outcomes from the LASW program.

Blythe and Allen's (1999) research on the LASW program found that teachers often talk about reflecting on student work in terms of assigning a grade to the paper. On the other hand, what students write down on their papers can be the key to understanding teachers' instructional methods and how teachers impact learning. Blythe and Allen (1999) stated that educational leaders must establish a community within their schools that allows for this reflection and learning. Additional research in this area has been completed by Langer, Cotton, and Goff's (2003) *Collaborative Analysis of Student Work*, in which they discuss a collaborative process for deeply examining a small number of students' work through a form of the LASW process completed over an entire school year. Both groups of researchers agree that collaborative reflection, on student work and teaching methods, enables teachers to learn from one another and creates an increase in the use of best practice within schools. This collaboration leads to an increase in resources, ideas, and strategies that make an individual teacher's efforts more productive.

Blythe and Allen (1999) found that for real change to occur within schools, stakeholders must create change from the ground up. This means there must be an effort to empower teachers and treat them as professionals. School administrators should provide opportunities for teachers to become leaders in the school, for example, through the use of teacher facilitators. Langer (2003) refers to this as establishing a culture of collaboration, arguing this is necessary for programs such as LASW to work and create the desired instructional changes.

• • •

References

American Federation of Teachers (2002). *Principles for professional development*. Washington, DC: American Federation of Teachers.

Alkin, M. C. (2004). *Evaluation roots; Tracing theorists' views and influences*. Thousand Oaks, CA: Sage.

Allen, D. (1995). The tuning protocol: A process for reflection. *Studies on exhibitions* No 15. Providence, RI: Brown University, Coalition of Essential Schools.

Allen, D. & Blythe, T. (2004). *The facilitator's book of questions: Tools for looking together at student work*. New York, NY: Teachers College Press.

Apollo Middle School Improvement Team (2010, March). *Apollo Middle School-- School Improvement Plan*. In possession of the researcher.

Association for Supervision and Curriculum Development (2002). *Examining student work facilitators guide*. Alexandria, VA: ASCD.

Blythe, T. & Allen, D. (1999). *Looking together at student work: A companion guide to assessing student learning*. New York, NY: Teachers College Press.

Bogdan, R. C., & Biklen, S. K. (1998). *Qualitative research for education* (3rd ed). Boston: Allyn and Bacon.

Coalition of Essential Schools. *Essential schools website*. Retrieved July 4, 2009 from http://www.cesnorthwest.org/cfg.php

Cushman, K. (1996). *Looking collaboratively at student work: An essential toolkit*. Horace, 13, 2, 2-4. Providence, RI: Coalition for Essential Schools.

Cushman, K (1998). *How friends can be critical as schools make essential changes*. Retrieved July 4, 2009 from http://www.essentialschools.org/resources/45

DuFour, R. & Eaker, R. (1998). *Professional learning communities at work: Best practices for enhancing student achievement*. Bloomington, IN: Solution Tree.

DuFour, R., Eaker, R., & DuFour, R (2005). *On common ground: The power of professional learning communities*. Bloomington, IN: Solution Tree.

DuFour, R., DuFour, R., Eaker, R., & Many, T. (2006). *Learning by doing; A handbook for professional learning communities at work*. Bloomington, IN: Solution Tree.

DuFour, R., DuFour, R., & Eaker, R.(2006). *Professional learning communities at work*. Bloomington, IN: Solution Tree.

Dunne, F., Nave, B., & Lewis, A. (2000, December). *Critical friends groups: Teachers helping teachers to improve student learning.* Phi Delta Kappa Center for Evaluation, Development and Research. Retrieved April 19, 2004 from http://www.pdkintl.org/edres/resbul28.htm

Eaker, R., DuFour, R. & DuFour, R. (2002). *Getting started: Reculturing schools to become professional learning communities.* Bloomington, IN: Solution Tree.

Felder, R. (2010). *Resources in Science and Engineering Education.* Retrieved July 4, 2009 from http://www4.ncsu.edu/unity/lockers/users/f/felder/public/RM F.html

Graham, B. & Fahey, K (1999, March). School leaders look at student work. *Educational Leadership,* 25-27.

Guskey, T. (2002). Professional development and teacher change. *Teachers and teaching: Theory and practice,* 8, 381-391.

Guskey, T. (2000). *Evaluating professional development.* Thousand Oaks, CA: Corwin Press, Inc.

Guskey, T. (1985). The effects of staff development on teachers' perceptions about effective teaching. *Journal of Educational Research,* 78, 378-381.

Guskey, T. (1985). Staff development and the process of teacher change. *Educational research,* 13, 63-69.

Guskey, T. (1991). Enhancing the effectiveness of professional development programs. Journal of educational and psychological consultation, 2(3), 239-247.

Guskey, T. & Huberman, M. (1995). *Professional development in education new paradigms and practices.* New York, NY: Teachers College Press.

Harmony Education Center (2009). *National School Reform Faculty*. Retrieved June 14, 2009 from http://www.nsrfharmony.org/faq.html

Kagan, S. (1994). *Cooperative learning*. San Clemente, CA: Kagan Publishing.

Langer, G., Colton, A., & Goff, L. (2003). *Collaborative analysis of student work*. Alexandria, Virginia: ASCD.

Lewis, A. (1998). Teachers in the driver's seat. *The Harvard Education Letter*. 14, 1-4.

Liebermann, A. & Miller, L. (2000). Teaching and teacher development: A new synthesis for a new century. *Education in a New Era; ASCD Yearbook* Virginia: *ASCD* 47-66.

Lindolf, T. R. & Taylor, B. C. (2002). *Qualitative communication research methods* (2nd ed). Thousand Oaks, CA: SAGE Publications.

Looking at Student Work Association (2009). *Looking at student work*. Annenberg Institute for School Reform. Retrieved April 2009 from http://www.lasw.org/

Lowden, C. (2006, Winter). *Reality check*. Journal of Staff Development. National Staff Development Council. 27, 61-64.

Patton, M. (2002). *Qualitative research & evaluation methods* (3rd ed). Thousand Oaks, CA: SAGE Publications.

Rademaker, L. (2008). Using qualitative observations to enhance the professional development program: What the numbers can't tell you. *Journal of Ethnographic & Qualitative Research*, 2, 205-211.

Stewart, J. & Neufled, B. (2000). *Standards-based reform in Corpus Christi; A focus on the early implementation of looking at student work*. Cambridge, MA: Education Matters.

Stufflebeam, D. L. & Shinkfield, A. J. (2007). *Evaluation theory, models & applications.* San Francisco, CA: Jossey-Bass.

Whitehurst, G. (2002). Improving teacher quality. *Spectrum: Journal of State Government, 75,* 12-15.

Yin, R. K. (2003) *Case study research: Design and methods* (3rd Ed). Thousand Oaks, CA: Sage Publications.

• • •

Appendix A: Collaborative Assessment Protocol

Developed by Steve Seidel and colleagues at Harvard Project Zero (www.lasw.org, June 21, 2009)

1. Getting Started

   • The group chooses a facilitator who will make sure the group stays focused on the particular issue addressed in each step.

   • The presenting teacher puts the selected work in a place where everyone can see it or provides copies for the other participants. S/he says nothing about the work, the context in which it was created, or the student, until Step 5.

   • The participants observe or read the work in silence, perhaps making brief notes about aspects of it that they particularly notice.

2. Describing the Work

   • The facilitator asks the group, "What do you see?"

   • Group members provide answers without making judgments about the quality of the work or their personal preferences.

   • If a judgment emerges, the facilitator asks for the evidence on which the judgment is based.

3. Asking Questions About the Work

- The facilitator asks the group, "What questions does this work raise for you?"

- Group members state any questions they have about the work, the child, the assignment, the circumstances under which the work was carried out, and so on.

- The presenting teacher may choose to make notes about these questions, but s/he is does not respond to them now--nor is s/he obligated to respond to them in Step 5 during the time when the presenting teacher speaks.

4. Speculating About What the Student Is Working On

- The facilitator asks the group, "What do you think the child is working on?"

- Participants, based on their reading or observation of the work, make suggestions about the problems or issues that the student might have been focused on in carrying out the assignment.

5. Hearing from the Presenting Teacher

- The facilitator invites the presenting teacher to speak.
- The presenting teacher provides his or her perspective on the student's work, describing what s/he sees in it, responding (if s/he chooses) to one or more of the questions raised, and adding any other information that s/he feels is important to share with the group.

- The presenting teacher also comments on anything surprising or unexpected that s/he heard during the describing, questioning and speculating phases.

6. Discussing Implications for Teaching and Learning

- The facilitator invites everyone (the participants and the presenting teacher) to share any thoughts they have about their own teaching, children's learning, or ways to support this particular child in future instruction.

7. Reflecting on the Collaborative Assessment Conference

   • The group reflects on the experiences of or reactions to the conference as a whole or to particular parts of it.

8. Thanks to the Presenting Teacher

• • •

Appendix B: Tuning Protocol

Developed by Joseph McDonald and David Allen (www.lasw.org, June 21, 2009)

1. Introduction (5 minutes)

   • Facilitator briefly introduces protocol goals, guidelines, and schedule

   • Participants briefly introduce themselves (if necessary)

2. Presentation (15 minutes)

The presenter has an opportunity to share the context for the student work:

   • Information about the students and/or the class — what the students tend to be like, where they are in school, where they are in the year

   • Assignment or prompt that generated the student work

   • Student learning goals or standards that inform the work

   • Samples of student work — photocopies of work, video clips, etc. — with student names removed

   • Evaluation format — scoring rubric and/or assessment criteria, etc.

   • Focusing question for feedback

- Participants are silent; no questions are entertained at this time.

3. Clarifying Questions (5 minutes)

- Participants have an opportunity to ask "clarifying" questions in order to get information that may have been omitted in the presentation that they feel would help them to understand the context for the student work. Clarifying questions are matters of "fact."

- The facilitator should be sure to limit the questions to those that are "clarifying," judging which questions more properly belong in the warm/cool feedback section.

4. Examination of Student Work Samples (15 minutes)

- Participants look closely at the work, taking notes on where it seems to be in tune with the stated goals, and where there might be a problem. Participants focus particularly on the presenter's focusing question.

- Presenter is silent; participants do this work silently.

5. Pause to reflect on warm and cool feedback (2-3 minutes)

- Participants take a couple of minutes to reflect on what they would like to contribute to the feedback session.

- Presenter is silent; participants do this work silently.

6. Warm and Cool Feedback (15 minutes)

- Participants share feedback with each other while the presenter is silent. The feedback generally begins with a few minutes of warm feedback, moves on to a few minutes of cool feedback (sometimes phrased in the form of reflective questions), and then moves back and forth between warm and cool feedback.

- Warm feedback may include comments about how the work presented seems to meet the desired goals; cool feedback may include possible "disconnects," gaps, or problems. Often participants offer ideas or suggestions for strengthening the work presented.

- The facilitator may need to remind participants of the presenter's focusing question, which should be posted for all to see.

- Presenter is silent and takes notes.

7. Reflection (5 minutes)

- Presenter speaks to those comments/questions he or she chooses while participants are silent.

- This is not a time to defend oneself, but is instead a time for the presenter to reflect aloud on those ideas or questions that seemed particularly interesting.

- Facilitator may intervene to focus, clarify, etc.

8. Debrief (5 minutes)

- Facilitator-led discussion of this tuning experience.

USING TODAYSMEET TO ENGAGE STUDENTS

• • • Jason Bretzmann • • •

SINCE PLATO PASSED A note in Socrates' class, students have been communicating in the backchannels of education. In my learning communities, I encourage students to send messages in the most high-tech way they can. We use www.todaysmeet.com to communicate in the backchannel. We also extend the reach of TodaysMeet by using it in other innovative ways, like sharing feedback about the class, displaying comments on class content, and extending the reach of the classroom. TodaysMeet creator James Socol supports the variety of ways his website has been integrated. "The most exciting part of TodaysMeet has been watching teachers invent new ways of putting the tool to use."

What is the Backchannel?

The backchannel is what happens behind the scenes in our classrooms, or during our presentations. It is what the students are thinking about under the radar as the main focus of the class takes place in the foreground. It's what they are saying under their breath, whispering when we turn around, and thinking about, either individually or collectively. It's the questions students have, the answers they discover, and the exciting ability they have to extend the lesson beyond the reach of the normal in-class activity. The backchannel *is* differentiation, collaboration, and critical thinking.

Why Would We Want Students to Communicate in the Backchannel?

The questions, answers, comments, and thoughts are happening, anyway. TodaysMeet helps bring them out into the open so they can be useful and enhance the educational opportunities of each student. I encouraged students to use the backchannel during my lecture to share questions, links, and comments on my questions.

One of the first times I used TodaysMeet was in an Advanced Placement class that included one very quiet student. Although the work that Stephanie turned in was good, I never really knew what she was thinking or if she was learning at a deep level. Her thinking and learning were on full display with TodaysMeet. With stealthy quickness, this one quiet girl answered my questions. I watched, but I couldn't even catch her doing it. She was a TodaysMeet ninja. She was the first to answer several times, while sharing her accurate and well thought-out comments. This girl had never said anything before, and now Stephanie was contributing in a substantive way and showing her deep understanding of the concepts. Maybe the backchannel allowed her to shed her shyness or gave her just enough anonymity to feel comfortable. Either way, TodaysMeet gave Stephanie the confidence to become more engaged in the class. It benefitted her and gave everyone a better experience.

With her added confidence, I saw Stephanie begin to participate out loud in class, as well. She really came out of her shell after the initial TodaysMeet experiences. It turned out that not only did she have a deep understanding of the content, but she had a great personality and a wonderful sense of humor. TodaysMeet and her own desire to participate allowed her to show those important attributes to the rest of her classmates.

I have also seen TodaysMeet allow for a real exchange of content ideas in the backchannel. During a lecture on money in politics, I mentioned that some candidates get money from PACs, figuring students knew what they were. I was wrong. A student asked his classmates, via TodaysMeet, what a PAC was. Though I was monitoring the backchannel on my iPad as I was lecturing, I hadn't noticed this particular question. By the time I noticed it, a classmate had not only answered the question, but he had also provided a link. The student and the rest of the class were able to access the information while I continued with the lecture. The question was asked and answered, and the learning experience had been enriched, not by me, but by the other learners in our community.

From the beginning, I tell students that we shouldn't even call it "the classroom." Instead, we have a learning community. I tell students that we are in this together and that we will construct our knowledge of the content as a group. I let them know that while I have important degrees, formal training, and a lot of experience, I can guide them in the right direction, but I am not the fount of all wisdom and knowledge. I tell my students if they want to pretend I know everything, they can also read my fictional and facetious book, *The Internet? I Just Finished Reading That.*

How Does It Work?

Todaysmeet.com is a very simple website. Its minimalism is akin to Google®. There is a dialogue box that asks you to name your room, and as you name it, the website gives you immediate feedback as to whether or not your chosen room name is available. If it's available, you can create your room immediately by clicking on "Create your Room." The default setting saves your room for one week. You can change the drop-down menu to keep your room active for as little as two hours or as long as one month. Once you have created your room, it shows up as its own TodaysMeet website. An example could look like www.todaysmeet.com/bretzchat103. Students, or anyone in the world, can then join your room. Participants don't use an e-mail, Twitter, or Facebook login. They simply choose a name by typing it into the dialogue box that asks "What's your name?" and then clicking "Join." I recommend that my students join with their first name and last initial. In that way, I know who they are, but we help avoid any unsavory characters that are trolling the Internet. Once they join, students can type up to 140 characters (like tweeting) and then click "Say." TodaysMeet creator Socol intended to make the process easy. "I created TodaysMeet so classes, meetings, or presentations would have a way of creating a backchannel that would be open to anyone with a web browser, regardless of whether they'd signed up ahead of time."

Sometimes it is helpful to display student comments, and sometimes it is better to have the backchannel behind the scenes of the class' main focus. It will depend on your learning objectives and what is needed for any given lesson or class. If you display comments, there is even a "projector" button that removes the dialogue box for comments and only displays the comments.

You can use this technology in a big computer lab, with a mobile computer lab of laptops, with bring-your-own-devices programs, with cell phones, or whatever creative way you can connect students with a web-enabled device. You'll be able to encourage your students to share questions, comments, answers, links, and feedback in real time. At the end of the process, you can assess who was commenting by clicking on the transcript tool at the bottom of the page and either printing it or making a PDF to save it for later.

What Happens the First Time People Use TodaysMeet?

I first saw www.todaysmeet.com used by author and blogger Will Richardson at a technology conference at a local high school. He told the teachers gathered in the auditorium that we could use TodaysMeet to communicate with the other people in the room, and we could share feedback with him while he gave his presentation. It was a liberating feeling to be encouraged to get connected and chat with other audience members while the presenter was talking. The process also transformed us from passive members of the audience into active participants in the exchange of ideas and information. We were part of the presentation.

What followed was almost a giddiness that revealed the excitement the participants felt. These were people who had sat through endless hours of professional development, enrichment, and, in some cases, patronizing presentations. Now, they were being asked to be actively involved. They responded with silliness at first. Teachers who knew each other joined the chat and acknowledged each other with comments like, "Hi, Sally, I see you sitting down there." Or "Hey, Bob, I can see your bald head shining up there in the front of the room." Some taskmasters eventually steered the conversation toward the presentation. "Hi, everybody. This is a really cool website. Looking forward to the day." Throughout the rest of the presentation, the participants shared thoughts, asked each other questions, constructed meanings together, and gave feedback to the presenter and each other.

I've found that this process is similar for both adults and students. The first time an audience or a class uses this technology, they spend some time in the silly space. Sometimes even those who haven't used TodaysMeet for a while will revert back to starting with the silly stuff.

In many cases, I've felt like I'm watching the gorilla at the zoo being offered a new ball. He grabs it, and tilts his head back and forth as he looks at it from several different directions. Then he paws at it and plays with it to see what it will do. Once satisfied that it's a good toy, he starts the serious work of using the ball for its intended purpose. Perhaps it is the nature of all animals to play around with something to see what happens before using it for its intended purpose. Perhaps my sociological and evolutionary analogy goes way too far.

In either case, I suggest that you should expect some playing around when you introduce TodaysMeet. Please don't be discouraged by that. Please don't put it away and think that your students "can't handle it." It may take some work on your part to get them to the next stage, but they can get there. You may have to set some expectations and guide them to where you want them to be. But always keep in mind that, whether they are adults or students, they will probably start out with fun, and you or someone in the class will have to maneuver them toward an effective use of this great tool.

What are Student Expectations for TodaysMeet?

It is always useful to set expectations for technology use in our classrooms. It is helpful for students to know what they will be using, what they should do with it, and what they should get out of it. The following are some general expectations I give to my students:

- Ask questions of each other.
- Answer each other's questions.
- Provide links to academic content when you can.
- Be respectful.
- Encourage the exchange of ideas.
- Extend each other's knowledge.
- Remember that everything you post will be seen by everyone, everywhere forever.

How Can We Use TodaysMeet for Feedback?

As part of my first steps into flipping my classroom, I wanted to find out what the students were thinking about the learning process they were going through and how well-prepared they were. So I asked them. Students went to www.todaysmeet.com/feedbackch1. They were asked to form groups of four, and each student was given a Chapter 1 test and answer sheet. Students discussed and answered the test questions, while simultaneously assessing their learning and commenting on TodaysMeet. In addition, I was able to comment and guide the students, re-direct them back to the focus of my questions, or answer incidental questions as they came up. One of my first comments was, "If you have comments about the effectiveness of the questions, please post them." I wanted students to evaluate the test questions based on their knowledge of the learning objectives. Four minutes later, I asked, "Do you feel prepared for the test?" In the next two classes, I adjusted and asked students first if they felt prepared for the test. This seemed like a more logical first question.

I had the questions typed out already, so I could just copy and paste them into TodaysMeet when I felt students were ready. In one of the classes, I was able to change the order of some of the questions because I had the questions prepared beforehand. This turned out to be even more useful the next day because a third of the students had been gone on a field trip the first day. When they came back, I was able to put them into a group together, set up a new TodaysMeet room and start them from the beginning of the feedback questions, while the other students continued where they left off the previous day.

Generally, students responded that they felt prepared for the test and understood some of the concepts very well. From my daily discussions with each student, I knew that they were prepared, but it was good for me and for them to write it down and share it with the world. They were publicly stating that they were knowledgeable. This is no small feat for some high school students who regularly feel like they have to justify why they know things, why they studied, or why they went beyond the graded materials.

When I asked if students had taken good notes, it was good to see that students honestly assessed their note-taking abilities and in some cases—without prompting by me—they made a plan to take better notes in the future. This would not have happened if we had engaged in a full-class discussion about better note taking or if I had asked out loud whether students had done a good job. They would not have had the time to reflect and communicate a thoughtful answer and consider a plan of action for the future. Many students would have allowed one or two students to respond and not felt the need to respond for themselves. TodaysMeet pushed each student to consider and communicate an answer.

Using TodaysMeet for feedback also gave me valuable information about the class. I thought the process we followed to learn the material was taking too long. From the feedback I got from students, I was able to cut out a portion of the discussion that the students (and I) thought was not as productive as it could have been. Working together and using TodaysMeet, we were able to learn more efficiently.

While getting feedback, the only minor technical glitch we had with TodaysMeet happened when one impatient student posted the same comment multiple times because he kept clicking the "say" button. I tried to keep the atmosphere light-hearted because the student was a bit embarrassed. After his tenth post showed up, I commented, "You can say that again, Jon."

How Can We Use TodaysMeet to Display Content?

Often in class, we want students to answer questions, to share meaning, or to construct meaning as a group. I observed a science teacher using TodaysMeet so her students could do all of those things. She asked the students specific questions about the scientific process and asked them to post their answers, which were displayed on the screen via the LCD projector. The students were able to answer the questions, find success, and make sure their answer matched up with what others were saying. As she walked around the room, the teacher pointed out some good responses, and the class was able to come to a common understanding of the answers to her questions. Then the teacher was able to ask why this was an important step in the process. She got a variety of responses to her open-ended question. Again, she moved around the room while highlighting good points that the students were making. They were able to construct meaning for each question as a group. They collectively created an extensive answer to a series of higher-level questions.

In my civics-oriented class called American Issues, I give a discussion quiz on the topic of power. Instead of writing answers to questions and handing them in, students discuss what they know. It is another way for students to show understanding without writing a paper and pencil test. After studying the concepts related to power, students are required to answer pre-determined questions in class. The class is split up into two groups, and each group sits in a circle on one side of the room. I ask a question to one side of the room; then I ask the same question to the other side, and they discuss the question, as well. Then I ask the next question to the side that just finished answering the first question. Next, we proceed back to the first group and then go back and forth through the 10 questions. In the past, many students who were on the side of the room that wasn't discussing were either irritated that they couldn't chime in on the other side's discussion or were not paying attention because they weren't required to comment at that time.

I leveraged the TodaysMeet technology to keep the discussion going and allow those who wanted to share more to do so. When it wasn't their circle's turn to discuss, students were able to continue communicating with the help of TodaysMeet. This was effective because some students couldn't get all of their thoughts out during their side's group discussion, either due to the amount of time I allowed or because shyness wouldn't let them add more. Some just needed a longer deliberation process before they jumped in with their two cents.

During the quiz, if students don't speak at all, they earn zero points. Students are required to speak once to earn 15 points out of 25. When students speak at least twice, their online comments add to their grade. Since speaking twice was the trigger that made the online comments count, it led to some uncomfortable students sharing their thoughts out loud more than they normally would have. Then, they added comments using TodaysMeet in a more comfortable online forum. This resulted in students sharing a little more out loud and sharing even more online. It gave them additional avenues to show their knowledge and pushed them a little out of their comfort zone.

While this wasn't the perfect process for every student, what followed was a more meaningful and rich discussion. Students not only displayed their content knowledge, but they also shared links to other content in order to extend the lesson and make it more relevant. As a testament to its effectiveness, it was energizing to be part of a discussion that evolved into students questioning the need for government, ambling through John Locke's ideas about why government is necessary, and leading to an exchange of student questions and links to information that went well beyond the intended lesson.

How Can We Extend the Boundaries of the Classroom?

As I mentioned, I start the year by telling my students that we are not a class, but a learning community. I add to that by saying that AP Government is not a course, but a way of life. With TodaysMeet, I have been able to extend the boundaries of our learning community and make what we do even more a part of my students' lives. During the presidential and vice-presidential debates, we were chatting live using TodaysMeet.

Chatting wasn't graded, assigned, or required. It was made available to my students so they could share their comments about the progress of the debate and engage in an analysis of the process in real-time with the rest of our learning community. It was a meaningful experience for these students as they shared a passion for government and politics with others who share the passion. They had each other at the TodaysMeet room to bounce ideas off of and to focus and refocus their discussion toward an academic end. Afterward, one student wrote, "It helped me hear other people's point of views on it while it was happening, and I believe that made me watch the debate with more of an open mind."

I started each debate chat session by posting the same "To Do" and "To Don't" list that I explained in class:

Do

1. Share comments based in fact
2. Share links to relevant sites
3. Stay focused on the topic
4. Discuss content-related topics
5. Analyze

Don't

1. Make stuff up
2. Focus on personalities, looks, or other irrelevant issues
3. Distract the group with extraneous ideas
4. Call people names
5. Paste "talking points"

I gave students two other bits of advice before the debates began:

- Remember: Every comment you make can be seen by everyone forever everywhere.

- Remember to use www.tinyurl.com to shorten links (it leaves more room for your comments!)

During the debates, some of my students from other classes even showed up to watch the chat. Several made comments. During the debates that took place from 8:00 to 9:30 at night, there were a total of 705 comments (a third came in the first debate).

Using the tools at the bottom of the TodaysMeet screen, I was able to switch to the transcript mode and create a savable PDF. From there, I published the students' comments and shared them as an e-book. I posted the e-book on my website as a student-created example that shows that young people, even those that can't yet vote, can be involved in the civic process of elections.

Having observed their behavior and maturity using TodaysMeet, I felt confident that my students were ready for a less controlled environment. When students asked if we were going to chat during the election results, I suggested they ask for parental permission to go to the nationally promoted #eduelection chat on Twitter. Many tweeted on election night with students and teachers around the country.

What is the Impact of TodaysMeet?

Since we have started using TodaysMeet, students have realized its usefulness. They have started to request TodaysMeet, and some students have taken it upon themselves to set up rooms so they can share content, comments, and questions with their classmates. The first time this happened, a junior student set up a room called todaysmeet.com/brodychat. He proceeded to post questions for his classmates, and he moderated the room like a twitter chat. As students worked in groups to understand the learning objectives, they were also answering his questions on TodaysMeet and asking questions of their own.

Using TodaysMeet in a variety of ways has helped to engage my students. Students have shared feedback to help improve their learning and my teaching. Students have displayed their knowledge of the content and confirmed the construction of their knowledge by comparing it to the learning of others. They have extended the learning beyond the lessons and beyond the school day.

TodaysMeet creator Socol adds, "When you build a tool, you have some idea of how it will be used, but, almost always, you only see a small part of the potential." With the help of TodaysMeet, my students have taken increased ownership of their learning and have been able to better understand their roles in our learning community. My students have become better learners and have learned more.

As in other learning communities, the backchannel is happening. In our learning community, my students and I use the technology to capture it and direct it for enhanced learning experiences. I like to think that if Plato were in my class today, he would share a link describing the poisonous chemical properties of hemlock. It sure would be informative, and I don't think Socrates would make him write an "apology" for doing it.

INFUSE OR EXCUSE

• • • Mark Walters • • •

AS WIKIPEDIA DEFINES IT, "technology is the making, modification, usage, knowledge of tools, machines, techniques, crafts, in order to solve or help solve a problem or achieve a goal." I suppose we'd all agree that what we have here is a fairly accurate definition of the word. My question to you is: Have *you* been using technology in the classroom? If so, for how long? When did you begin? How did you begin? When did technology really become a dominant force in education?

Approximately ten years ago, a teacher in the school in which I was serving at that time shared with me an observation report he had just received on a grammar lesson he had presented—his "write-up," if you will. The write-up, in many aspects positive, hit a negative tone when the observer (subject chairperson) suggested that the teacher did not use "technology" during the course of the lesson. Reference was made to the fact that there were in the back of the room five or six laptop computers (then a fairly new phenomenon) which students could have used during the course of the lesson to research various parts of speech, etc. The teacher explained to me that the chairperson was indeed correct—there was no use of the laptop computer—but there was indeed "technology." He used the overhead projector, a tape recorder, truth-be-told, an old film strip and film strip projector, and a VHS tape being played in a VCR (remember them?). The students also used pens, pencils, and wrote on something formerly known as papyrus. There seemed to be plenty of 'technology' in that room. Yet, the chairperson indicated that there was no use of "technology!"

What was he trying to say—there was no use of technology—or no use of the computer—current technology?

I started teaching in 1962, and I always found that the kids loved it when I used my 45/LP record phonograph, the overhead and opaque projectors, the Wollensak reel-to-reel tape recorder and other such "contraptions." They truly enlivened my lessons, and I became known as "Mr. Gadget." I made regular use of the mimeograph machine, as well as the blue ink spirit duplicator, known as the Rexograph (wow—the kids loved to take a whiff of that spirit ink—not to mention some teachers, as well!). These were the tools, machines, techniques, and crafts I used to help solve a problem—that problem being: how to best get my message across. It was *my* TECHNOLOGY. I didn't call it technology—but it most certainly was. It was just as much technology as was the first chisel used millennia ago, the first piece of slate used for ancient folk to write upon, or the first quill. I have no doubt in saying that after the wheel was invented, someone nearby must have exclaimed, "What won't they think of next?"

So here I am writing a chapter dealing with instructional teaching techniques and strategies. Well, here's a strategy. Let's start talking straight with our kids. The dumbing down of America has got to end somewhere—and let that ending begin with us. I say that when we talk to our kids—when we instruct them—we had better strategize to know just what we are talking about. What a disservice we do our kids when we say something like, "Well, we have to infuse technology into the lesson." Infuse technology? Wasn't the teacher using a blackboard, a piece of chalk? Weren't the kids using pens and pencils? Wasn't the classroom light on? Did you see any candles, pray tell? And who knows, maybe if this had been a lesson taught in the 16th century—or even 18th—there, indeed, would have been a candle lighting the desk—so the student could see what his/her quill was writing!

Teachers! Administrators! All Educators! Stop this nonsense NOW! If you want a teacher to use a computer in the lesson, then say, *"I want you to infuse the computer into your lesson"* —rather than, *"I want you to use technology in the lesson."* Or you can suggest that you would like the teacher to use "current technology" in the lesson. Our students deserve to "hear it right;" we owe them that much.

And—oh yes, let's not forget this one: *We are living in "modern times."* Just what exactly is meant by "modern times?" Are we referring to NOW? How do we define "now?" Is it today, yesterday, last year? Is it this decade, this quarter or half century? Is "tomorrow" just as "au courant" as "today?" Would it not better serve us and our students to say: *We are living in current times*— the word "current" being a bit more synonymous with "immediate?" Haven't all "times" been—at one time or another— "modern?" Pre-historic times were "modern" back in the day, before there *were* "times." The middle ages were once modern times. When? In the Middle Ages!

Using wrong terms and expressions such as "modern times" and "technology" reminds me of those who regularly—no, constantly—say to kids: *stop eating so many fries—they're not healthy for you—you should eat healthier foods, such as broccoli and tomatoes.* Well, have you ever seen a healthy tomato or a stalk of broccoli that looked in perfect health? Have you ever asked an apple how it felt? Sure, we hear it regularly on radio and television, but does that give us the right to teach our kids "the wrong" instead of "the right?" Why can't we all say "healthful," instead of "healthy?"

Why can't we talk "right" to our kids—so our kids will talk "right" to us?

ENDANGERED SPECIES

• • • Lana Turner Wilson • • •

IMAGINE FOR A MOMENT, you are a young African American male sitting in a fourth-grade classroom. You are not interested in the lesson that is being taught because you cannot make a connection. You are tired of sitting in your seat for such long periods of time, so your legs ache and your mind wanders. You feel your teacher does not believe that you can do good work and is not interested in what you think. How would *you* feel? What would *you* do? After serving in education for over 20 years, I have witnessed African American males slipping through the cracks of the educational system and dropping out, despite legislative and judicial efforts to promote educational equality and success.

In 1954, the Oliver Brown v. the Board of Education of Topeka (KS) United States Supreme Court decision was a significant milestone to promote equal educational opportunities for African American students. In 2001, the "No Child Left Behind" (NCLB) Act was a framework for bipartisan education reform to increase accountability for states, school districts, and schools. The Investment Act of 2009 funded the "Race to the Top" contest, created to promote innovation and reform in state and local district kindergarten to 12th grade education. These factors have not eliminated the academic achievement gap between African American males and other students. Today racial, social, and gender issues in education remain, and large numbers of African American males are not *racing to the top* of the honor roll. They are being *left behind*.

African American males are an "endangered species" because they are disappearing. Without the appropriate literacy skills and support, many African American children are being prepared for life on the streets and will subsequently experience violence, unemployment, prison, and death. I have observed a disproportionate number of young African America males who are being referred to special education programs and are suspended or expelled from school. Students who are suspended are more likely to fall behind their peers academically. If these students do not receive counseling, encouragement, and consistent instructional support, they will be retained more frequently than other students. A mentoring program with adult African American males to serve as role models would be optimum.

Currently serving as an instructional coach in a large urban school district, I have observed white and African America teachers who were quite successful at meeting the academic needs of young African American males and others who were not academically successful. There existed a distinct pattern of teacher characteristics and instructional practices among the successful teachers. These teachers were positive, caring, and had high expectations for all of their students. They worked hard to promote their students' self-esteem. They were reflective about their instruction and used assessment to set and adjust instructional goals. These teachers were able to bridge cultural barriers, as well as maintain a positive and respectful classroom climate. They built mutual trust with their African American male students by structuring a classroom environment where it was safe to take risks and make mistakes in order to learn. These successful teachers' instructional practices for young African American males included many of the following ten characteristics:

- African American culture and masculine themes were used as an important instructional resource to build on the young males' prior knowledge and foster a positive sense of identity.

- Teachers taught lively and relevant cooperative learning activities that promoted active student involvement and often included a "competitive spirit."

- Lessons included activities for students with kinesthetic and visual learning styles.

- Strategies were taught so students could independently apply them to handle cognitively demanding tasks, and hence, take responsibility for their own learning.

- Teaching was appropriately paced to optimize clarity, instructional time, and promote student engagement.

- Learning tasks, outcomes, new information, and directions were clearly communicated to the students, with opportunities to ask questions.

- Constructive feedback on students' work was shared in a timely manner and academic success was vigorously celebrated.

- All students experienced rigor through access to relevant problem and project-based learning activities that stimulated critical thinking.

- Students' progress was regularly monitored through a variety of assessments to differentiate instruction to meet individual needs.

- Struggling students were provided with extra instructional support and extra time, if needed, to complete assignments.

Based upon my personal teaching practices and observations of other teachers, I have concluded that text choice for young African American male students can be quite critical to their engagement in instruction and literacy success. They seem to prefer highly relevant nonfiction texts about real events, new knowledge, and situations that emphasize masculinity. Their dominant fiction interests were science fiction, scary stories, and reading about other young males (preferably African American) in real-life situations. Regardless of genre, most young males seem to enjoy themes that include animals, motor vehicles, science, sports, airplanes, food, and video games. When given a choice, graphic novels, anime, and comic books are often selected by young males. I strongly believe that biographies of successful and heroic African American males can be useful tools to inspire young males and help develop their pride and sense of social justice.

Providing quality literature for students to select and take home is immensely important. Negative and inappropriate images of African American males in the mass media and violent video games are often providing children with entertainment, instead of appropriate literature to read at home. It can be difficult for some parents to buy an engaging selection of books for their children to read at home. If the library is a distance from home, the streets can sometimes be too dangerous to go to the library.

All students deserve and require quality literacy instruction by highly qualified and caring teachers. Teachers who have the "Missionary Disorder" and pity African American students and lower instructional rigor are not helping them. African American males' literacy achievement gap will never close if they do not receive the strategic instruction and intervention that respects their culture and gender. There are African American males (as young as fourth grade) who have lost hope in education and are looking for more immediate gratification in the streets by engaging in dangerous and destructive activities. Also, they meagerly populate institutions of higher education. This is a travesty in a country that has an African American male president. We could be losing future teachers, doctors, or inventors.

Some could argue that making deliberate instructional decisions to support African American males is unnecessary, because they must adapt in order to effectively assimilate into the larger society. However, astute and successful educators understand that strategic differentiated instruction is a tool to meet the instructional needs of all students. Strategies that are shared in this essay can be used to teach all students. Consistently implementing strategies that could enhance the literacy skills and self-esteem of African American males could save lives and subsequently help eradicate the "extinction" of African American males.

PAT QUINN

• • • The RTI Guy • • •

PAT QUINN HAS SPENT HIS entire career helping struggling students become successful in school. As a teacher, author, and nationally recognized keynote speaker, he has changed thousands of lives through his insightful message. Pat Quinn helps educators around the country improve their teaching, renew their passion, and lengthen their careers as he speaks about closing the achievement gap and meeting the needs of all students.

Mr. Quinn is the author of twelve books on meeting the individual needs of students, including *Ultimate, RTI, Helping Hispanic Students Succeed, Designing an Alternative Curriculum,* and the bestselling *Changing Lives*. He has taught undergraduate courses for Lakeland College and graduate courses at Alverno College. He is the former editor of the educational newsletter, The Unconventional Teacher.

To subscribe to Pat Quinn's RTI newsletter, visit:

www.response-to-intervention.com

Email Pat Quinn at: pat@betterteachingonline.com.

Made in the USA
Columbia, SC
21 September 2020